Telling the Story of Jesus

Faith and Understanding Series

Many people, both Christians and others, have very good and legitimate questions about the Christian faith. This series is designed to address some of those contemporary questions. The series features modest-length books designed for non-specialist readers—average "people in the pews" rather than theological students or seminary graduates. Each book gives the reader the basics of the subject matter, and a bit beyond the basics. The authors seek to open doors for readers to learn more about Christian faith and life—and why it matters in contemporary society.

Telling the Story of Jesus

The Gospel of Matthew for the Twenty-First Century

Sheila E. McGinn

FOREWORD BY

Aaron M. Gale

CASCADE *Books* • Eugene, Oregon

TELLING THE STORY OF JESUS
The Gospel of Matthew for the Twenty-First Century

Faith and Understanding

Cascade Books
An Imprint of Wipf and Stock Publishers
199 W. 8th Ave., Suite 3
Eugene, OR 97401

www.wipfandstock.com

PAPERBACK ISBN: 979-8-3852-6742-2
HARDCOVER ISBN: 979-8-3852-6743-9
EBOOK ISBN: 979-8-3852-6744-6

Cataloguing-in-Publication data:

Names: McGinn, Sheila E. [author]. | Gale, Aaron M. [foreword writer].

Title: Telling the story of Jesus : The Gospel of Matthew for the twenty-first century / by Sheila E. McGinn ; foreword by Aaron M. Gale.

Description: Eugene, OR: Cascade Books, 2026 | Series: Faith and Understanding | Includes bibliographical references.

Identifiers: ISBN 979-8-3852-6742-2 (paperback) | ISBN 979-8-3852-6743-9 (hardcover) | ISBN 979-8-3852-6744-6 (ebook)

Subjects: LCSH: Bible.—Matthew—Commentaries. | Bible.—Matthew—Criticism, interpretation, etc.

Classification: BS2575.52 M34 2026 (paperback) | BS2575.52 (ebook)

VERSION NUMBER 04/29/26

Emphasis added to Scripture quotations.

In gratitude for all the unnamed women and men disciples of Jesus, from the early Matthean community down to the present day, who helped create and continue to exemplify this story we love to tell

In loving memory of Mary Katharine Deeley, who both lived and told this story well

I love to tell the story!
'Twill be my theme in glory
to tell the old, old story
of Jesus and his love.

—William Gustavus Fischer

CONTENTS

OUTLINE

ABBREVIATIONS

1 En.	1 Enoch
ANF	*Ante-Nicene Fathers*
AT	Author's translation
AYBRL	Anchor Yale Bible Reference Library
BRev	*Bible Review*
Gos. Pet.	Gospel of Peter
Gos. Thom.	Gospel of Thomas
JSNT	*Journal for the Study of the New Testament*
JSNTSup	Journal for the Study of the New Testament Supplement Series
Kil.	*Kil'ayim*
LCL	Loeb Classical Library
Ned.	Nedarim
NPNF[1]	*Nicene and Post-Nicene Fathers*, 1st series
NPNF[2]	*Nicene and Post-Nicene Fathers*, 2nd series
RBS	Resources for Biblical Study
Šabb.	Shabbat
Šeb.	Shevi'it

FOREWORD

DR. SHEILA MCGINN BRINGS over thirty years of expertise to this current volume. I am proud to have known her for much of that time, and we share a common interest regarding the history and message contained in Matthew's Gospel. In fact, it was Dr. McGinn who suggested that I write on the literacy of the Matthean community for my master's thesis at John Carroll University, which turned out to be the catalyst for my own career of over twenty-five years as a Matthean scholar.

The evolution of contemporary Matthean scholarship itself has resulted in diverging lines of thought regarding the First Gospel, especially since the publication of Krister Stendahl's *The School of St. Matthew, and Its Use of the Old Testament* in the mid-1950s. Latter twentieth-century scholars continued to debate and reformulate Matthew's meaning and social context, particularly as it relates to issues such as feminist readings, anti-Semitic interpretations, and the subsequent relationship of the text to contemporary Christian discourse. Therefore, a quarter way through the twenty-first century it is more prudent than ever to synthesize and summarize current trends in Matthean scholarship, which this volume seeks to do in several ways.

Dr. McGinn notes that the primary aim of this volume is to shed light upon the Gospel for lay readers who are interested in learning more about Matthew's history and meaning. Yet the text also provides for the reader a basic (and readable) summary of current academic theories related to the First Gospel, which the most established of scholars will also find very helpful. The first chapter, for example, provides for the reader the latest information regarding Matthew's origins, date, and location, as well as explaining the text's proper place within the canon (it was likely not the first gospel).

The commentary itself is especially valuable due to its unbiased correction of previously problematic assertions, such as the accusation that the text is the most anti-Semitic of the four canonical gospels. Anti-Jewish readings of Matthew's Gospel still abound, and anti-Jewish interpretations continue to be found in passages such as the infamous blood-cry in Matt 27:25 ("His blood is on us and on our children"). Scholars continue to debate Matthew's very connection to the laws of the Torah and to Judaism itself. Readers will appreciate McGinn's clear and concise attention to these issues, as in her notes relating to 5:13–48, where scholars have often claimed Jesus abolishes the Torah and its laws. In reality, the reader is made to understand that Jesus upholds and elevates the Torah laws, while providing additional commentary on them for his followers.

Perhaps most intriguing is Dr. McGinn's attention to the integral role of women within the First Gospel. As early as chapter 1, she points out for the reader the unique inclusion of women within Matthew's genealogy, and continues to correct the common patriarchal interpretations of the narrative that have been adopted through the centuries. As McGinn herself notes, "Without the women disciples of Jesus, there would be no story to tell." This is illustrated at times by Jesus himself, who attempts to prevent the abuse of women through his very teachings, as McGinn points out in her interpretation of the antitheses. Furthermore, she clarifies the prominent role of women within this Gospel, most clearly illustrated in her treatment of the Canaanite woman in Matt 15:21–28. Ultimately, McGinn notes the overall bravery of the women disciples, who themselves could have faced a gruesome fate for remaining by Jesus's side during his crucifixion (see her notes on chapter 27), yet chose to keep vigil for him.

This volume also goes beyond many other commentaries by providing a "life beyond authorship" ending for the reader. The last chapter in this commentary focuses on Matthew's primacy within the context of the early Christian world, particularly as it relates to Mark's Gospel and other early texts such as the Didache. There is a reason for Matthew's preeminence, and McGinn carefully explains to the reader why this is so through the utilization of helpful primary sources (e.g., Ignatius of Antioch and Eusebius). She makes a convincing case that Matthew's Gospel was the lens through which the other gospels were viewed due to its placement first within the canon as well as its cornerstone teachings.

Ultimately, McGinn's provocative commentary elicits a contemporary and exciting reading of Matthew's Gospel that readers at all levels will find intriguing and thought-provoking. In addition, her review and discussion questions serve as place cards for continued dialogue, and they help to situate the reader within the framework of the first-century Jewish–Christian world. Questions such as "Who finally was responsible for Jesus's execution?" would no doubt have been asked by Jesus's first followers. McGinn's commentary thus links the past to the present and reminds her audience that a new and innovative interpretation of Matthew's Gospel deserves to be heard in the twenty-first century.

—Aaron M. Gale

West Virginia University
Morgantown, West Virginia

ACKNOWLEDGMENTS

ANY BOOK LIKE THIS represents the influence and work of many people, not only the author. There is no way to thank all the many colleagues and students who, over forty years of teaching, have helped shape this volume. My parents and maternal grandmother introduced me to Jesus and the gospel stories about him, walking and talking with me all along the way as I questioned and grappled with making that story my own. In my university days, Professor Edmund Perry sparked my interest in the historical person, Jesus of Nazareth, and—perhaps unbeknownst to him—set my feet on the path of following that story as a teacher and scholar. Father John Krump took that story of Jesus and made it real in his preaching every week at the Northwestern University Sheil Center. Professor Rosemary Ruether took seriously the interest of a fresh-faced teenager in the women around Jesus and helped foster and hone that interest with solid research skills. To them and to so many others of happy memory, my deepest gratitude.

Several colleagues have been conversation partners on the subject matter for decades. Mary Katharine Deeley and Aaron Gale are foremost among those, but the list also includes Professors Raymond Collins, John Dominic Crossan, Amy-Jill Levine, Frank Matera, John P. Meier, Barbara Reid, and many others too numerous to mention. This book is better because of them.

As always, my two adult children and my one-and-only favorite sister have served as cheering section along the way. I cannot thank them enough for putting up with me talking too much about the project and for helping me think through how best to approach the various issues in ways that would make sense to a typical reader.

Sincere thanks also go to Frank Hughes, coeditor of this new Faith and Understanding series, who honored me with the invitation to join him as general editor and to kick off the series with this Matthew volume. I can only hope the resulting book lives up to that trust.

Finally, I would like to thank Rebecca Abbott, Shannon Carter, and Calvin Jaffarian, of Wipf and Stock, for their generous help in making this book a reality. Rebecca was a tremendous copy editor, both eagle-eyed for every detail and helpful with overall style questions. Shannon generated the beautiful cover design, for this book and for the Faith and Understanding series. And Calvin is the most efficient proof editor I have ever worked with. All of them have made the actual publication phase of this project a breeze.

INTRODUCTION

THIS BOOK IS DESIGNED for readers who are interested in learning what we know about the Gospel according to Matthew, what "story" of Jesus it tells (especially in comparison to the other gospels), and what contemporary readers might care about those questions. The volume might serve as a refresher for those pursuing academic investigations of the Bible, but it is designed for the average reader more than those engaged in formal biblical studies.

Those who identify as Christians might be expected to find this exploration of GMatthew of value, but the author also hopes it will be of interest to those who identify as "spiritual but not religious." Building upon chapter 2 of Frank Hughes's recent volume on Mark,[1] this book takes a new look at GMatthew in light of current archaeological and historical studies to see where the evangelist's story of Jesus fits with the author's own time and place in late first-century Judaism and how that might matter to twenty-first century readers.

Overview of This Volume

This book is divided into ten chapters, the first nine of which follow key divisions to GMatthew itself. Chapter 1 outlines the strategy for this exploration and provides background information key to understanding GMatthew in its sociohistorical environment. Chapter 2 explores the infancy narrative (Matt 1–2), which serves as an overture to the entire Gospel. This is followed by one chapter for each of the five "books" within GMatthew,

1. Hughes, *Guide to Mark*, ch. 2, "Why and How to Study the Gospels."

which focus on key sections of the teaching of Jesus that the evangelist has collected into "sermons." So, chapter 3 focuses on the inauguration of Jesus's ministry and the first discourse, known as the Sermon on the Mount (Matt 3–7); chapter 4 explores the mission of Jesus and his followers, concluding with the mission discourse (Matt 8–10); chapter 5 addresses Jesus's strategic choice to use parables to convey his vision of the reign of God, and concludes with the parabolic discourse (Matt 11–13); chapter 6 explores GMatthew's presentation of Jesus as founding a renewed community of Israel, which concludes with the discourse on the church (Matt 14–18); and chapter 7 reviews the evangelist's invitation to readers to prepare for the final age, with particular attention to the discourse on the end-time (Matt 24–25). Chapter 8 focuses on the passion and resurrection narratives (Matt 26–28), the climax and culmination to the story GMatthew tells. Chapter 9 summarizes the fundamental perspectives raised in GMatthew and points to the future impact of this Gospel in emerging Christian discourse. Finally, chapter 10 addresses what is called the "reception history" of this Gospel, that is, how GMatthew was used in the early Christian discourse of the decades soon after it was written.

While occasional biblical verses are quoted in full, the reader will want to have a Bible—or at least GMatthew—open while going through this text.

Each chapter includes a brief study guide with review notes and discussion questions for use in a bible study setting. The chapters are followed by a brief conclusion, reprising the significant points of this volume, and a list of other works of potential interest to readers.

Terminology

As you will have noticed, I am using GMatthew to refer to the gospel book. This is to help readers remember that this gospel comes down to us from an unknown author or group of authors. In the second century, early Christians assigned the name "according to Matthew" to this gospel and speculated that the author was one of Jesus's original disciples, whom they viewed as a former tax collector for the Roman Empire (e.g., Matt 9:9; 10:3). However, we have no external historical evidence for that attribution, and it is exceedingly unlikely that this supposition is correct. A tax farmer would not have had the extensive knowledge of the Jewish Scriptures and their interpretation necessary to produce the refined theological arguments that characterize this gospel. Jesus might have made converts from among those Jews who originally allied themselves with the oppressive Roman regime, but it does not follow that such disciples would have the educational background to produce GMatthew. Most scholars today view this gospel as the product of a group of Christ-believing scribes, not any one individual. So, I will refer to the authors as the Matthean scribes or the Matthean community and will use GMatthew to denote the product of their theological reflection on the divine revelation made manifest in Jesus of Nazareth, whom they viewed as the long-awaited Messiah of Israel.

Basic Tools and Strategies

More will be said later about specific methods of reading GMatthew, but a few comments are important to set the stage. We will be analyzing pre-gospel materials and exploring comparisons between GMatthew and the other gospels that have come down to us, especially GMark and GLuke.[2] Even a cursory review of these three gospels shows that they have similar storylines and share some specific scenes and stories. Their similar viewpoints have led to them being classed as "Synoptic" Gospels. The extensive similarities among the three gospels raise the question of what is called literary dependence. When phrases and even entire stories are repeated word for word and the texts are not quoting from the same external source, standard rules of literary analysis suggest that one of the versions must be the original and the others later copies or revisions of it.

Signs of literary dependence include:

1. Structural similarities (e.g., matching outlines and/or timelines)
2. Matches in narrative content
3. Identical phrasing
4. Unusual technical terms or idiosyncratic language that matches across versions

As we'll see below, all four of these types of literary dependence appear when comparing the three Synoptic Gospels.[3]

2. The technical word for surviving materials is "extant," i.e., those that still exist today.

3. Sometimes we also see examples of what is called "editorial fatigue," when later authors include borrowed material that contradicts editorial changes they made elsewhere in the text. This evidence of literary dependence is more frequent in plagiarized student papers than in the Synoptic Gospels.

How do we determine which is the earliest version? Again, the same basic rules apply to all sorts of texts, not just those of the gospels.

1. Generally speaking, shorter texts are earlier. This is especially true when looking at religious texts that the audience sees as divinely revealed. Editors would not want to omit anything that might be important to the divine message.[4]
2. The more difficult version tends to be earlier. The text might fit this category because it contains one or more misspelled words or a phrase is grammatically awkward. It may describe a relative location or an itinerary that is geographically improbable or even impossible. More seriously, when looking at religious texts, sometimes a "difficult" text is one that poses theological problems that the editor deems necessary to eliminate.[5]

These rules are not applied woodenly, but they allow for a consistency in analysis that is important to reliable scholarly work. We will discuss the consensus on interrelations among the three Synoptic Gospels in chapter 1. For now, it is sufficient to note that these guidelines for discerning literary dependency underlie those conclusions.

Reading the Text in Its Contexts

In addition to this basic kind of analysis of the relationship of the texts with each other and with the other available source materials, a responsible reading strategy requires understanding the text against the background of its wider literary, historical, and social contexts. Such a responsible reading takes more work than the surface reading people do, but it is the only way to allow the text to speak for itself rather than making the text mean whatever the reader wants it to say. Unlike popular parlance, which claims that the surface reading is a "literal" reading, the contextual reading is what actually provides the literal meaning of a text (i.e., the meaning that fits its literary form and cultural context).

4. This is not the only reason GMark is viewed as the earliest of the Synoptic Gospels, but it is a key factor. See ch. 1 for a fuller discussion.

5. In the New Testament, a text that shows Jesus's ignorance seems to pose an embarrassment to the later evangelists. Similarly, the later synoptists do not like the fact that Jesus began as a disciple of John the Baptist (compare Mark 1:9–11 vs. Matt 3:13–17 and Luke 3:21–22), while GJohn eliminates the baptism scene altogether (John 1:29–34).

Literal*ism* pretends that such concerns don't matter to texts, but we know from common experience that it matters quite a bit.

The same words carry different meanings depending upon the type of literature in which they appear, that is, according to their literary form. For example, Ps 76:2 says that "God's tent is in Salem." The literary form of the psalm (poetry) cues us that this is a metaphorical expression concerning the divine presence and peace, not an assertion concerning God's physical, geographical location. Similarly, when Gen 49:9 calls Judah "a lion's cub," it would be ridiculous to take this literalistically, as if the author was claiming Judah belonged to the species *Panthera leo* rather than *Homo sapiens*. No, the *literal* meaning of each of these texts is its poetic, metaphorical reading. The same is the case with key terms concerning Jesus in the gospels (e.g., "lamb" of God, "son" of God). A careful reading distinguishes such metaphors rather than "dumbing down" the New Testament texts.

In addition to these kinds of contextual differences that affect meaning, time also has an impact. Language changes meaning over time; the same words carry different meanings depending upon their literary, social, historical, and cultural contexts. For example, when Thomas Oliphant first wrote the lyrics to the Christmas carol "Deck the Halls" (in 1862), he had no idea what the phrase "gay apparel" would imply in the twenty-first century, nor that the verb "deck" would convey a violent act.

Similarly, when the New Testament evangelists called Jesus "the Christ," they could not imagine what the fourth-century church would do with that language in the Nicene Creed, nor what the fifth-century Council of Ephesus would assert in the two-natures doctrine. Contemporary readers of the gospels reflexively read into the New Testament texts later meanings of terms like the title Christ. Such superimposition makes the biblical texts mirror the readers' preconceptions instead of respecting the gospels as revelatory texts from first-century Christ believers.

If we want the New Testament to speak the good news to us today, we must carefully and responsibly attend to what such terms meant to the *original* audiences for whom these texts were written. For many, this will be the most difficult aspect of reading this book, but it remains the most valuable aspect of the work involved in reading the Bible. If we accept that the Bible conveys the divine word, we have to get ourselves and our preconceptions out of the way so it can speak on its own terms. We have to do the work to uncover, as best we can, what the texts meant to their original audience, instead of reflexively falling into a literalistic reading with meaning superimposed by the contemporary reader. That *original* meaning constitutes an authentic *literal* reading of the texts.

Review and Discussion Questions

A. Review Questions

1. Who probably authored GMatthew?
2. Which are the "Synoptic Gospels" and why are they classified that way?
3. What are the signs of literary dependence? Which ones do we find when comparing the Synoptic Gospels?
4. According to the author, what constitutes a literal reading of the biblical text?

B. Discussion Questions

1. What has been your earlier experience of reading or studying the Bible?
2. Is the approach in this book different from your earlier Bible study experiences? What might be the benefits of this way of reading?
3. Why is it important to read the biblical texts in their original historical and cultural contexts? What can happen when readers fail to take that original context into account?

Chapter 1

GMATTHEW IN ITS SOCIO-HISTORICAL ENVIRONMENT

The "First" Gospel Is Not the First

GMatthew appears first among the canonical gospels for theological reasons. This kind of editorial choice is fairly common in the Bible. The most familiar case appears in Gen 1–3, where the two stories of creation are placed chronologically backwards so readers will interpret the older story (Gen 2:4b–3:24) in light of more recent theological developments (represented in Gen 1:1–2:4b). Similarly, in the New Testament, GMatthew appears before the oldest of the gospels (GMark) so readers will construe the image of Jesus in GMark in line with the newer gospel—which, as will be argued later, was designed to replace that earlier narrative.

Another theological factor has to do with establishing a relationship between the two Testaments of the Christian Bible. GMatthew refers to the prophetic books of the Old Testament so frequently, it was viewed as creating a bridge from the Old Testament to New Testament. Contemporary Christian Bibles place the book of the prophet Malachi last in the Old Testament and GMatthew first in the New Testament. This makes a solid theological connection between the two Testaments: Malachi focuses on the coming of the Messiah and the reign of God while GMatthew presents Jesus as that promised Messiah who inaugurates the reign of God.

GMatthew Builds on GMark

How do we know that GMatthew is a later work than GMark? Comparing the two gospels shows that over 75 percent of GMatthew comes from GMark.[1] Of this material adopted from the earlier gospel, the authors of GMatthew made various changes and adaptations to fit with their specific community situation in the mid-80s CE, which was based either in the Syrian metropolis of Antioch-on-the-Orontes or in the Galilean environment near the rather cosmopolitan Herodian city of Sepphoris.[2] In either case, we are dealing with a much more affluent population than the community of GMark, as can be seen from some of the changes made to GMark by the scribal community of GMatthew.

In addition, GMatthew recontextualizes the story of GMark by adding the infancy narrative and extending the resurrection narrative; adding significant sections of teaching of Jesus (organized as five main discourses, which we will discuss in chs. 3–8); omitting characterizations of Jesus that may be viewed as negative (e.g., avoiding mention of Jesus's impatience or frustration [Matt 12:12 vs. Mark 3:5; and Matt 12:39 vs. Mark 8:12]; eliminating Jesus's subordination to John the Baptist [Matt 3:13–17 vs. Mark 1:9–11]); and correcting a sense that Jesus's message is aimed primarily—or exclusively—for the poor and relatively powerless (e.g., the addition of "in spirit" in the first macarism at Matt 5:3). GMatthew also presents Jesus's family of origin as more favorably inclined toward his mission; this gospel also generally presents Jesus's women and men disciples in a more positive light than GMark—a feature especially notable in the resurrection narrative, which presents the women disciples obeying the angelic command to take the message to their "brothers" rather than fleeing in fear (Mark 16:8a vs. Matt 28:8).

In theory, all of these changes could go the other direction: GMark could make the disciples look more inept, Jesus more insecure and fearful, etc., but those kinds of modifications stagger the imagination. Why would

1. Similar statistics are true of GLuke, but that's a topic for a different book. For those who are visual learners, two helpful diagrams are available from Naselli, "Structural Difference."

2. Ancient Sepphoris in Galilee is modern Tzipori, Israel, while Antioch-on-the-Orontes is contemporary Antakya, Turkey. The two cities are just under 380 miles distant from each other—about two weeks' travel time on foot or by donkey cart.

Aaron M. Gale has been among the advocates for a Galilean provenance for GMatthew, although not necessarily Sepphoris itself. See, e.g., Gale, "God, Galilee, and Gospels"; *Redefining Ancient Borders*, esp. ch. 2.

someone create a new "gospel" that makes Jesus and the disciples look worse than one that already exists? The common guidelines for discerning this kind of literary dependence suggest that a later editor would correct such awkward situations, improve the grammar, and make other logical (and, in the case of religious materials, theological) corrections to the text. Thus, scholars for centuries have viewed GMatthew as a more developed gospel, both in the literary and theological sense; and, for over a century, there has been a strong consensus that GMark is the first of the canonical gospels with GMatthew (and GLuke) building on that earlier literary work.

Other Sources for GMatthew

GMatthew has access to other sources for material about Jesus besides GMark. One of those sources is known as Q, short for the German word *Quelle* (which simply means "source").[3] This refers to the set of sayings of Jesus reported by both GMatthew and GLuke but not GMark. Some modifications have been made to this hypothesis since it was first suggested in the nineteenth century, but the basic outlines have remained the same.[4] Contemporary scholars agree that GLuke tends to preserve the earlier versions of Q sayings, since the Lukan versions of the sayings tend to be shorter and more pointed than the versions in GMatthew.

Another source used by the authors of GMatthew is denoted M (for "Matthean material") and refers to sayings unique to this gospel. This collection includes the parables of the tares (Matt 13:24–43), the hidden treasure (13:44), the pearl (13:45–46), and the dragnet (13:47–52); the unforgiving servant (18:21–35); the workers in the vineyard (20:1–16); the two sons (21:28–32); and the ten virgins (25:1–13). One might think that M should include the infancy narrative, since most of its details are unique to GMatthew, but these are narrative materials rather than sayings

3. Johannes Weiss is the German scholar who first used this term and abbreviation to refer to the collection of sayings shared by GMatthew and GLuke but not found in GMark (*Predigt Jesu*, 8).

4. Burnett H. Streeter made an early and influential development to the Q hypothesis, including that it was written in Koine Greek and that the versions in GLuke tend to be closer to the original than those in GMatthew (*Four Gospels*). One of the most influential twentieth-century proponents of Q has been John Kloppenborg, who views it as a (now lost) written source that went through three editions over decades in the middle of the first century CE (*Q, the Earliest Gospel*).

attributed to Jesus. The unique details of the Matthean infancy narrative will be addressed in the next chapter.

The final source for GMatthew is the Jewish Bible in its Greek translation, known as the Septuagint (abbreviated LXX). GMatthew, which is written in Koine Greek, quotes extensively from the Greek version of the Jewish Bible (not the Hebrew Bible). There are a few places where the Septuagint translation differs somewhat from the Hebrew version of the same biblical book, and GMatthew always follows the Greek text.[5] As we will see, the gospel makes the most use of Psalms and the prophetic books, but there also are images drawn from the Torah and other parts of the wisdom literature.

Unlike the Q and M source material, GMatthew's use of the Jewish Bible shows extensive theological reflection upon those materials. The scribal community that produced this gospel scoured their Bible for texts that would help them understand the significance of Jesus and God's revelation through him. They then shaped these biblical sources to create their own exposition of the "good news" of and about Jesus taking off from GMark but modifying it in significant ways.

Why Was This Gospel Composed?

Since GMatthew was not the first gospel, and those who composed it already had GMark available for their use, one must ask why they would bother writing this new gospel. Why did the Matthean community not simply use the gospel text already available to them? No doubt, a number of factors were involved in this decision, but the bottom line is that they intended to replace GMark with their new gospel. They disagreed with some of the ways Jesus was portrayed in GMark, and there were aspects of his life and mission they thought deserved more—or less—attention than GMark gives to them. They accepted the basic timeline of Jesus's ministry as outlined in GMark, but they were not satisfied with the way GMark begins (with Jesus becoming a disciple of John the Baptist) nor with the way it ends (at Mark 16:8a, with the faithful women fleeing the tomb in fear rather than taking the resurrection message back to the other disciples). If these two features of GMark

5. Perhaps the most well-known locus is the text from Isa 7:14. The LXX translation says, "A virgin shall conceive and bear a son," whereas the Hebrew text of that verse reads, "A maiden shall conceive."

come as a surprise to you, it shows how successful the Matthean community was in replacing the image of Jesus presented in GMark.

I do not mean to suggest that the Matthean community's revisions to the image of Jesus were arbitrary or intended to mislead. As we saw in the previous section, they had access to two sources of sayings of Jesus (Q and M) that were not available to the Markan community. In addition, they appear to have had a number of scholars well acquainted with the Jewish tradition and trained in various methods of interpretation of the Jewish Bible. The quality of writing in GMatthew shows a higher level of education than that represented by GMark, and some of the details in the gospel suggest the Matthean community was more affluent than the one for whom GMark was written. The scribal circle who composed GMatthew no doubt saw themselves as correcting errors that had been overlooked by those who had composed the earlier gospel.

The Matthean Community and Their World

Who belonged to the Matthean community and what was their world like? Some general outlines can be gleaned from the contents of the gospel. The text shows extensive familiarity with the Torah, Prophets, and Jewish Wisdom writings (especially Psalms) in their Greek translation. Such scholarship requires a stable environment with the financial resources to host a library of biblical scrolls. Publishing any book in antiquity required hiring a scribe to make a fair handwritten copy of the text, and then getting several more scribes or a scriptorium to make hand copies of that original.[6] As you can imagine, this made books quite expensive, so only affluent persons could afford them.[7] In addition, literacy rates were about 5 percent; only the wealthy could read and write. Thus, we have two indicators that the Matthean community was relatively affluent: they could afford a scriptural library, and they could support scholars in their work of researching the biblical texts to find what message was hidden there to help them understand what new thing God had done through Jesus.

6. The first use of a moveable-type printing press in the Western world was the Gutenberg Bible, printed in 1450. Moveable type was invented in China several centuries earlier, and the *Diamond Sutra* (ca. 866 CE) is widely viewed as the earliest published book, but that took place over 750 years after GMatthew was produced.

7. It takes a scribe nearly a year to make a Torah scroll; costs for community-size Torah today range between $30,000 and $100,000. The entire collection of the Torah, Prophets, and Writings could easily cost $250,000.

Such capabilities argue for a rather prosperous and sophisticated city location, not a small town or village. The two most viable locations are Sepphoris, the capital of Galilee rebuilt by Herod Antipas soon after the death of his father (Herod the Great, ca. 74–4 BCE) and Antioch-on-the-Orontes, the capital of the Roman province of Syria (founded ca. 300 BCE by Seleucus I Nicator, a former general of Alexander the Great).

Sepphoris has the advantage of proximity to the primary nexus of the ministry of Jesus; it lies ca. 100 miles from Jerusalem, but only 8 miles from Nazareth and 25 from Capernaum, where Jesus made his home in later years. Having been destroyed by the forces of Herod the Great after the uprising under Judas the Galilean (ca. 6 CE), the inhabitants of Sepphoris did not join in the Jewish revolt against Rome (66–73 CE). They withstood two attempts at conquest by the rebels led by Josephus. When the Roman legate Cestius Gallus led a force (including the Legio XII Fulminata) from Syria into Galilee, the troops were welcomed in Sepphoris and the inhabitants pledged their support of Rome. After the Jewish revolt was suppressed, Sepphoris benefited both culturally and economically from their loyalty.

Antioch, on the other hand, is substantially removed from all three key cities (ca. 400 miles from Jerusalem, 375 from Nazareth, 380 from Capernaum). With a population numbering perhaps 250,000, it was among the four largest cities in the first-century Roman Empire. An old, established city and center of commerce reaching not only around the Mediterranean region but as far away as China, it had a well-established Jewish quarter in its southern section. It boasted not only the famous paved Roman roads, city walls, and aqueducts, but also a theater, several public bath complexes, and a hippodrome (track for chariot races) to rival the Roman Circus Maximus. Certainly, the Jewish population there had more than sufficient resources to support a project like this gospel.

What about security? One might think it would be safer for Jews living in Syria during the revolt, but this was not always the case. While Syrian Jews were not directly involved in the uprising, anti-Jewish reprisals took place in individual cities, including Damascus, where a large number of Jews were lynched. When Titus Caesar visited Antioch in 71 CE, he faced a mob demanding that he expel the Jews; Titus refused, but the case shows the anti-Jewish sentiment of some segments of the population. So, while we might have expected the distance from Judea to provide some protection, this was not always the case. Antioch certainly was prosperous and had a substantial Jewish population dating back to its original foundation under Seleucus Nicator, but there might have been more disruption there than in relatively quiet Sepphoris.

In short, either location presents a viable option for the provenance of the gospel.[8] Sepphoris had more of a "new town" flavor, with a newly built palace, arsenal, city walls, and newly paved Roman roads to aid in communication and commerce, while Antioch was an historic center of trade, commerce, communications, and culture. New cities tend to be more future oriented and open to innovation and development, while populations in older cities tend to value lasting traditions and hereditary relationships. The Jesus tradition has a foot in each type of world, including "treasures both old and new" (Matt 13:52).

Conclusions

GMatthew was written to correct and replace the Gospel according to Mark, which the Matthean community had available to them. The scribal group who composed GMatthew also had available a sayings source (Q) and an independent collection of parables (M), which they incorporated into this gospel. While following the basic outline of the earlier GMark, they added introductory material (in the infancy narrative) and supplementary (post-resurrection) material at the end of the gospel to reframe the story of Jesus in a way that better suited the educational and evangelistic needs of their community.

While we cannot be sure of the Matthean community's geographic location, we do know that they were predominantly Jewish and had sufficient material resources to support a group of scribes while they researched the Jewish Scriptures and the traditions from and about Jesus of Nazareth. They valued intellectual pursuits, especially with regard to their religious heritage, and fostered a Jewish scribal culture in conversation with the wider Greco-Roman world and in the Greek language that predominated in their region of the Roman Empire.

The community members were sufficiently well educated to appreciate various nuances of the biblical texts and different modes of Jewish interpretation. They also were highly motivated to find such nuances in support of their interpretation of Jesus as a devout Jew, an expert interpreter of the Jewish Scriptures, a person obedient to Torah and faithful to the divine will to the very end. In fact, they were convinced that, because

8. Provenance refers to the geographic location where a work was produced.

of that faithfulness, what looked like the end for Jesus was not God's final word on the subject.

But we're getting ahead of the story. GMatthew sets up that ending by beginning at the very beginning, with a pre-story of Jesus called the infancy narrative.

Review and Discussion Questions

A. Review Questions

1. Why is GMatthew the first gospel in the New Testament?
2. Who produced GMatthew, when, and why?
3. What earlier source materials were used in the composition of GMatthew?

B. Discussion Questions

1. What do you think of the differences identified between GMatthew and GMark (e.g., the Sermon on the Mount, the post-resurrection appearances of Jesus)? What would the Christian life be like if we did not have this additional material (especially the Beatitudes, the Lord's Prayer, the final judgment scene)?
2. What elements of the Matthean story of Jesus resonate the most with you? Which do you find most challenging to understand or accept?
3. What difference does it make to think that this gospel was written primarily for Jewish Christ believers and by scribes trained in biblical studies and Jewish traditions? How might it change our understanding of Jesus and the early Jesus movement?

Chapter 2

THE INFANCY NARRATIVE

Overture to GMatthew (Matt 1–2)

THOSE READERS WHO ARE musically inclined will recognize the term "overture," which I've used here to describe the opening story of GMatthew. Originally employed by Raymond Brown in this context, an overture begins an orchestral work, presenting the major musical themes that will appear throughout the piece.[1] Unlike a medley, where the themes of different songs are strung together one after the other, an overture integrates the various musical elements of the ensuing piece, weaving them together nonsequentially, in ways that highlight their individual features while developing their interconnectedness. Thus, Brown's choice of terms in regard to the infancy narratives is perfectly apt. These opening chapters of GMatthew integrate all the key themes of the gospel, from Jesus's Jewish roots through his ignominious death at the hands of the political powers in control of the Jewish homeland. While a story about a child, the infancy narrative is not a children's story.

The "overture" nature of the infancy narrative demonstrates that the purpose of this section of GMatthew is theological, not historical. The ancient authors are setting the stage for understanding Jesus, and they use ancient art forms so their audience will grasp the significance of the story of Jesus. Here, in the infancy narrative, they incorporate themes of the ancient Greco-Roman romance novella: the relationship between Joseph and Mary, the threat of their separation, Joseph overcoming that

1. Brown, *Birth of the Messiah*.

threat and taking Mary as his wife; the birth of their child yields portents of future fame, but present opponents (Herod and his minions) threaten the child's survival; the holy family escapes to a foreign country and, after a sojourn long enough for the threat to die out (literally, with the death of King Herod), they are able to return to their homeland, at which point the novella concludes and the more historical aspect of the gospel begins (in ch. 3).[2] Like the other ancient novellae, the infancy narrative in GMatthew seeks to edify the audience while entertaining, conveying the key theological themes of the gospel while introducing a story the audience will love to hear—and then to tell.

The Book of the Genealogy of Jesus Messiah, Son of David, Son of Abraham (1:1–17)

The gospel begins with a genealogy, tracing the ancestry of Jesus of Nazareth through watershed figures in Israelite history. Starting with Abraham, the progenitor of the chosen people, the narrator traces Jesus's lineage through King David, the era of the Babylonian Exile (with indirect hints at Cyrus, king of Persia), and down to "Joseph, the husband of Mary." The genealogy is stylized into three sets of fourteen generations, hinting at the scribal authors' propensity for numerology: 3x14 = 6x7, which means Jesus is born at the beginning of the seventh seven, a hyper-perfect number. Jesus is called "Son of David," thereby placing him in the lineage of great Israelite kings. Although not named, Cyrus of Persia is the monarch who conquered Babylon and ended the Judeans' exile there; he is the only individual whom any Old Testament book names as "messiah" (Isa 45:1), so the genealogy thus hints at messianic role for Jesus as well. Jesus will liberate captives, like Cyrus did, and has ruling authority, like David had.

The specific language of the genealogy also hints at a "new creation" motif. The opening phrase, "these are the generations," repeats the language that concludes the cosmic creation story in Gen 1:1—2:4a, "These are the

2. Joseph and Asenath (by an unknown Jewish author) and *Callirhöe* (or *Chaereas and Callirhöe*, by Chariton) are two of the more famous ancient novellae. Asenath includes clearly Jewish theological themes while the latter represents a "secular" Greco-Roman story. See Brooks, *Joseph and Asenath*, for translation and commentary; see also the eminently readable précis and discussion of Asenath by Patricia D. Ahearn-Kroll, "Joseph and Asenath." See *Callirhöe*, in Reardon, *Collected Ancient Greek Novels*, 17–120.

generations of the heavens and the earth when they were created."[3] With Jesus, not only is Israel saved; the entire creation is being made new.

Many have noticed the oddity of women being included in this genealogy. Five mothers are included: Tamar, Rahab, Ruth, Bathsheba (indirectly named, she is "the wife of Uriah"), and Mary. All of the women were subjects of dubious stories. Commentators have suggested that the inclusion of the first four women as progenitors of the great kings of Israel (David and Solomon) serves to contextualize and undercut the rumors about Mary and Jesus's parentage. They also show that God can do great things through anyone God chooses, including those born into poverty and conflicted situations.

The genealogy names Mary as mother of Jesus and Joseph's wife, but does not claim Joseph as the father of her child (1:16). This omission is not remedied in the ensuing verses but instead is reinforced (e.g., 1:18–20). Unlike GMark (which tells us nothing of Jesus's birth and presumably thinks nothing worth saying about his parentage), the authors of GMatthew want to ensure that the audience knows Jesus's birth was miraculous, due to specific divine intervention. Allusions will later be made to earlier miraculous births like those of Isaac, Moses, and Samuel. The genealogy sets the scene for those later comparisons.

The Birth of Messiah Jesus (1:18–25)

The opening line of the birth story, "Now this is how the birth of Jesus Christ came about" (Matt 1:18a NABRE), constitutes a formula like "once upon a time." The authors tip the audience that, while not a "fairy tale" in the dismissive sense, the story they are about to tell is not history. Of course, Jesus was a historical figure actually born at the end of the first century BCE, but the Matthean story of that birth interweaves mythical elements with figurative meaning. John Dominic Crossan has used the expression "prophecy historicized" to describe the way the birth story and ensuing scenes were developed by the scribes who wrote this gospel.[4] They creatively used Hebrew prophecies and other biblical materials to

3. Some translations modify the language to "story," presumably on the theory that the heavens and earth cannot have "generations," but that undermines the precision of the Hebrew phrase and the parallel the authors of GMatthew were trying to create.

4. See, e.g., Crossan, *Jesus*, 145.

create an engaging story that conveys the truth of Jesus Messiah, a story one would love to tell.

The Matthean community knew that Jesus was God's promised Messiah of Israel; yet Jesus did not meet the expectations many Jews had of their messiah: he did not reestablish the Davidic monarchy nor drive the Roman overlords out of the Jews' ancestral homeland. Since Jesus, the true Messiah, did not meet these expectations, the ideas must have been mistaken; the messianic prophecies must have been misunderstood. How then should they be understood? What is the correct way to understand the significance of the birth, life, and ministry of the Messiah? These questions could be answered only by researching the Scriptures, rereading and reinterpreting them in light of the actual events of Jesus's life. That's what Crossan means by "prophecy historicized." The Matthean scribes worked backwards from the events of Jesus's life to find where the Scriptures explained their significance.

So, the Matthean birth story draws repeated connections between Jesus and important figures of Jewish history. Like his namesake in Gen 37–50, Jesus's father Joseph is a dreamer. Yet these dreams are better than those of his ancestor because they need no interpretation—an angel clearly conveys God's message in the dreams. There's a greater than Joseph here. Mary is named after Miriam, sister to Moses, who likewise was a savior to the Israelite people; yet there is a greater than Moses here. The prophetic quote from Isa 7:14 originally spoke of the birth of King Hezekiah, a faithful and righteous ruler who fought idolatry and restored the temple; yet there is a greater than Hezekiah here. All these ancestors are brought to witness in favor of Jesus as God's promised Messiah, who makes God's presence manifest: Emmanuel.

The Magi (2:1–12)

The first chapter of GMatthew sets Jesus in the context of Jewish history; ch. 2 begins to introduce the wider world, naming King Herod the Great as the ruler when Jesus was born and mentioning "magi from the East" (Matt 2:1). Christmas carols and pageants talk about "three kings," but there's no evidence of any particular number of magi, and magi are not kings. Magi is the masculine plural of magus, so there were at least two members of this group, and at least one was a man, but it might have been a mixed group, large or small. Persian priests were called magi, so "the East" here probably means that region, which includes contemporary Iran and Iraq. Mentioning the magi certainly shows the importance of non-Jews to God's messianic plan, and it also may hint back to Cyrus, the Persian messiah-king.[5]

As was frequently the case with ancient priestly roles, the magi's duties included astronomy and interpretation of heavenly omens. The story here speaks of a new star (2:2), which is among the omens thought to presage the birth of a great figure.[6] The authors of GMatthew would laugh to be asked what kind of star appeared. That's the wrong question. Jesus was a divinely sent figure, and God keeps the devout informed of divine plans. Speaking of a heavenly portent is the way to create a story the audience would love to tell.

The magi anticipated the birth of a king, so the story has them going to the king's house. But here it takes a twist: King Herod knows nothing of this birth, for it's not a son of his house. Herod is fearful of this unknown usurper, and his priestly advisers confirm the threat by citing Mic 5:2, which speaks of (the usurper) David's birth in Bethlehem. Herod follows with a closed-door meeting with the magi, acting as if he wants information about the child so he can recognize him as heir to the throne. The original audience of this story would know this for a blatant con. Herod had killed several of his wives and sons because he feared they were trying to usurp his throne; he certainly would not give way to an unknown village boy.[7] Every good story needs a villain, and Herod makes an apt choice for the Matthean story.

The magi make their way to Bethlehem with their rich gifts symbolic of royalty and priestly status. Again, these are features of the right kind of story. No evidence of these resources appears anywhere else in the entire gospel, and the original audience would not credit them as historical. Divine providence protects these righteous gentiles who have come to honor the messiah of Israel. Instead of returning to their home by the same route, an angelic message in a dream warns them to take a different way. God is supposed to protect the righteous and devout, so this element of the story reaffirms that stance. It also may hint at the fact that the way

5. See above, p. 10.

6. Similar language is used in the birth stories of Caesar Augustus; see Virgil, "Eclogue 4"; and Suetonius, *Augustus* 94. Again, we are not being told history here; theology is put into a story the audience would love to tell.

7. Herod executed his wives Mariamme I and Alexandra; his brother-in-law, Kostobar; and his sons Alexander, Aristobulus, and Antipater, the last who was killed in 4 BCE, the very year Jesus was born. See Flavius Josephus, *Antiquities* 17.1–5.

of Jesus, presented later in the gospel, is a different path than the one that leads to Jerusalem.

The Flight to Egypt (2:13–15)

Immediately upon the exit of the magi, we hear that Joseph has another dream, which brings an angelic warning about the devious Herod. The key purpose of this vignette is revealed in the final quote from Hos 11:1, "Out of Egypt I called my son." The Hosea text refers to Israel and the exodus, but the Matthean community uses it to highlight Jesus as representative of the whole people of Israel and to hint at "new exodus" imagery that will appear later in the gospel.

The Massacre of the Children (2:16–18)

The implicit threat of the previous scene becomes explicit in this vignette about the massacre of the children. The Matthean audience has no reason to love Herod, who died four generations before this story is being written, but they were not the only Jews who thought him despicable.[8] The Jewish historian Flavius Josephus tells a horrendous story of Herod's final illness and his plot to ensure that the people would mourn his passing.[9] A small section is worth quoting by way of comparison to this vignette:

> Now any one may easily discover the temper of [Herod's] mind . . . by those commands of his, which savoured of no humanity: since he took care, when he was departing out of this life, that the whole nation should be put into mourning, and indeed made desolate of their dearest kindred, when he gave order that one out of every family should be slain: although they had done nothing that was unjust, or that was against him; nor were they accused of any other crimes.[10]

Josephus was writing in the 70s, about the same time the Matthean community might have begun composing this gospel, which they published in the 80s. The antipathy against Herod clearly comes across in both tales, the one from Josephus and the one in GMatthew. Neither is likely to

8. Herod also took serious action against the Pharisees in 6 BCE, a group with whom the Matthean community had many affinities.

9. See Flavius Josephus, *Antiquities* 17.6, esp. 17.6.5–6.

10. Flavius Josephus, *Antiquities* 17.6.6.

be historical, but they establish Herod as the perfect foil for the story of Jesus. The evil king represents everything Jesus is not, and the threat to the child Jesus intimates the violence the adult Jesus will undergo at the hands of the designated rulers who succeed to power after Herod.

The Return from Egypt (2:19–23)

The final vignette in the infancy narrative begins with yet another angelic message in a dream telling Joseph to lead his family out of Egypt to the land of Israel. The exodus imagery reminds the audience of their ancestors' liberation from captivity under the leadership of Moses, implicitly establishing a comparison between Jesus and Moses (which will become explicit later in the gospel).[11] The mention of a continuing threat from the Judean power structure (v. 22) reminds the audience that the adult Jesus will have trouble there. Also, the Matthean community knows that Jesus was known as a Nazorean and that his ministry was based in Galilee, so this journey scene serves the purpose of getting Jesus to the right location to begin the narrative of his adult ministry.

Conclusions

The infancy narrative uses figurative language filled with engaging imagery to introduce the promise of Messiah Jesus as well as the threats against him and his divinely authorized message of salvation. As an overture to the gospel, it highlights key themes like the comparisons between Jesus and his ancestors David and Moses. It points the way for a positive reception of Jesus by gentiles (like the magi) and his rejection by the Judean powers that be (like Herod). The atrocious behavior imputed to Herod the Great in the massacre scene, while not historical, predisposes the audience to anticipate unjust treatment of the adult Jesus by another arbitrary and unjust ruler (Pontius Pilate). The journey motif sets the mood for the itinerant ministry of Jesus and keeps the Moses comparison in the forefront of their minds as the Matthean community begins to relate the story they love to tell.

11. For more comparisons between Jesus and Moses in the infancy stories of Exod 1–2 and Matt 1–2, see Crossan, "From Moses to Jesus."

Review and Discussion Questions

A. Review Questions

1. What are the unusual features of GMatthew's genealogy of Jesus? Why did the Matthean scribes include this in the introduction to their gospel?
2. GMatthew includes several distinct features in the infancy narrative compared to GLuke. What are a few of those distinct elements?
3. What do the stories of the magi and the flight into Egypt convey about Jesus's identity and significance?

B. Discussion Questions

1. The original audience of GMatthew would have read the infancy narrative as a romantic tale like the ancient romance novella of Joseph and Asenath. Have you ever thought about the romantic elements of the infancy narrative? How does it make you feel to think of it as a romance? How do you hear the story differently when you think of it through that lens?
2. What is lost when contemporary readers misread the infancy narrative as history? How does the readers' focus shift (e.g., from theology to claims about facts)? Does it take the excitement out of the story? Does it make it harder to relate to the characters?
3. What do you think about the inclusion of the few women in GMatthew's genealogy of Jesus? Why are they important to understanding Jesus's heritage, who and where he comes from? If you typically find genealogies boring, does it help to think of it as a sort of résumé, showing Jesus's ancestral "credentials" for the job of Messiah?

Chapter 3

JESUS INAUGURATES HIS MINISTRY

(Matt 3–7)

GMatthew is organized into five "books" of teachings from Jesus, following the pattern of the Torah as comprising the five "books of Moses." This first "book" in Matt 3–7 introduces the adult Jesus and his divinely authorized message of God's ruling authority and plans for recreating the world. This message is typically referred to as the proclamation of the "kingdom" or "reign" of God. Given the long anti-monarchy history of the USA, such language may be difficult for Americans to grasp and is worth explanation.

The Greek word used here is *basileia*, the term everyone in the ancient world used when referring not to geography but to the ruling authority of a monarch. In Jesus's day, the first response would be to think of the Roman emperor and imperial appointees. In other words, Jesus's proclamation of the coming *basileia* of God would be heard as a direct challenge to the existing *basileia* of Rome.

Fifty years later, the Matthean community had to confront the fact that Jesus did not overthrow the Roman government or drive the imperial agents out of the land of Israel. In fact, the great revolt against Rome (66–73 CE) had failed. Whether we envision GMatthew as written in Sepphoris or Antioch, either location would have included survivors from both sides of the failed revolt. The gospel writers needed to shape their story to unite the community behind Jesus's message, not to cause more division.

They all believed in Jesus's divine mission, which meant his proclamation had to be true. Thus, any earlier understanding of Jesus's message as anti-Roman must have been mistaken. The Matthean scribes shaped the message of Jesus to convey this "corrected" vision of what they believed Jesus must have meant when proclaiming the coming perfection of God's ruling authority.

Opening Scenes (Matt 3–4)

The Preaching of John (3:1–12)

GMatthew begins the ministry of Jesus not with Jesus himself but with John the Baptist. GMatthew follows GMark in noting that Jesus's first notable public act was meeting John, but GMark recognizes that Jesus became one of John's disciples. The Matthean community does not like the idea of Jesus being subordinate to John, so they adapt this scene to shape a different message: John is a "forerunner" to Jesus, not his master or leader.

GMatthew has John introduce the message of the coming *basileia*, here couched as "the kingdom of the heavens." The slight change of language has two purposes: to prevent inappropriate use of the divine name and, as mentioned above, to prevent the audience getting the wrong idea about a purely earthly reality that would challenge the authority of imperial Rome. Jesus's message has earthly implications, but the Matthean community wants to prevent it being heard as a political manifesto. Previous generations had done so, and it turned out to have been a deadly mistake.

John preached a baptism of repentance, that is, a change of life to return to the heart of Torah obedience. John himself is portrayed as a particularly pious man under a Nazirite vow, so he presents a stellar example of the truly obedient Jew. His "baptism" in the Jordan River replicates Israel's entry into the promised land. Those who pass through this water rite take upon themselves the challenge of Joshua to the people of Israel who survived the exodus and wilderness sojourn: "Choose today whom you will serve. . . . As for me and my household, we will serve the Lord" (Josh 24:15).

The Baptism of Jesus (3:13–17)

Jesus was baptized by John; everyone knows that. GMark admits this meant Jesus became John's disciple for a time; Jesus branched out on his own only after John was thrown into prison. The Matthean community is worried that this might lead people to think Jesus took orders from John, rather than directly from God. If Jesus is the true Messiah, he cannot be subordinate to John. So, the Matthean scribes rework the baptism story to highlight John not as Jesus's superior but as a witness to Jesus as Messiah:

> Then Jesus came from Galilee to John at the Jordan to be baptized by him. John tried to prevent him, saying, "I need to be baptized by you, and yet you are coming to me?" Jesus said to him in reply, "Allow it now, for thus it is fitting for us to fulfill all righteousness." Then he allowed him. After Jesus was baptized, he came up from the water and behold, the heavens were opened, and he saw the Spirit of God descending like a dove [and] coming upon him. And a voice came from the heavens, saying, "This is my beloved son, with whom I am well pleased." (Matt 3:13–17 NABRE)

The Matthean Jesus overcomes John's resistance by affirming that this baptism, which renews the person's commitment to live according to Torah (i.e., to live in righteousness) indeed does have that effect, even for Jesus (and, by implication, Jesus's followers as well). It does not make Jesus a disciple of John; rather, it renews Jesus's commitment to God.

A heavenly voice affirms the depth of Jesus's relationship to God by calling him "my beloved Son." Unlike in the Markan story, the voice speaks to John, not to Jesus; the Matthean community wants to convey that Jesus already knew his status in relationship to God.

Contemporary readers tend to have many misconceptions about this "sonship" language. I hope it goes without saying that it has absolutely nothing to do with biology. The Matthean scribes are thinking of the coronation psalms (e.g., Pss 2:7–8; 110), which call the Israelite king God's "son" and affirm that power and authority belong to him. By calling Jesus God's son, the Matthean scribes are affirming that, just like his royal ancestors, Jesus has the authority to speak and act for God.

To be named "beloved" son constitutes legal inheritance language. The beloved can act with full authority of the absent parent, controlling all property and assets. To be named regent for God is to be given authority over the creation generally, but especially over the land of Israel and the chosen people. In other words, the more important term in this formula is not "son" but "beloved." The heavenly voice affirms that Jesus is in fact the promised Messiah, with all the rights belonging to the true monarch of Israel. The Matthean community portrays John, the "forerunner," as the first to realize this. That makes a story they love to tell.

The Temptation of Jesus (4:1–11)

Hard on the heels of the baptismal revelation of Jesus's status as divine emissary comes the temptation scene. Will Jesus let this divine authority go to his head? Is he after political power for himself? Does he want to become "JC Superstar"? Or will he remain faithful to his baptismal commitment to covenant faithfulness and obedience to God? The temptation scene sets the audience members' minds at rest by raising and answering these questions.

The scene is set in "the desert," not a place like the Sahara or Death Valley; simply a spot that is uninhabited and therefore free of distractions. The language hearkens back to Israel's wilderness period, presented both as a time of testing and as a "honeymoon" period when the chosen people relied entirely on divine providence for sustenance. By focusing on the "tempter" as protagonist, the Matthean community highlights the "test" aspect of that period: "Remember how for these forty years the Lord, your God, has directed all your journeying in the wilderness, so as to test you by affliction, *to know what was in your heart: to keep his commandments, or not*" (Deut 8:2). Is Jesus a faithful Jew or a puffed-up self-promoter grasping for power? GMatthew uses this scene to show that Jesus truly is faithful to God.

The three temptations Jesus faces relate to miracle-working power ("command these stones to become loaves of bread" [Matt 4:3]), a test of divine providence ("throw yourself down" from the temple parapet [4:6]), and a test of true worship ("All these I will give to you, if you will fall down and worship me" [4:9]). Throughout the scene, the tempter quotes the Scriptures to justify his point of view, while Jesus presents an alternative text to challenge and correct the faulty interpretation. Knowledge of the Scriptures alone is not sufficient to show obedience to God; heartfelt devotion and reliance upon God are essential to a correct understanding. The tempter knows the words, but Jesus knows the heart of the biblical texts.

After passing the final test of gaining wealth and power through idolatry vs. living in faithfulness and worshiping the one true God, Jesus claims authority over the tempter. He commands the spirit to depart, and it obeys. In GLuke, we are told this is temporary (Luke 4:13), but the Matthean community wants to show a clear victory here. The accuser departs and "angels came and waited on [Jesus]" (Matt 4:11). Like the faithful of Israel whom God preserved through the wilderness, Jesus is preserved by God through this period of testing.

Jesus Begins the Ministry in Galilee (4:12–17)

Having demonstrated Jesus's complete obedience to God and—at least as important to the Matthean community—his skill at correctly interpreting the Holy Scriptures, the story turns to the beginning of Jesus's work as a public preacher and teacher. Note that Jesus takes this step only after hearing that John the Baptist has been imprisoned (Matt 4:12). The location of Jesus's public debut is not Jerusalem, the heart of the Jewish homeland and of temple worship, nor anywhere in Judea, but the northern region of Galilee, where shepherds, farmers, and fishers predominate the scene. Jesus was raised in Nazareth, but we hear that now he made his home in Capernaum (4:13; 9:1), a thriving town along the northern coast of the Sea of Galilee.[1]

Jesus's choice of Galilee as his home base conveys several important details about how he understood his mission. First, he was not focused on gaining political power or networking with those who had "clout." If he were, he would have had to set up shop in Jerusalem. Second, he did not affiliate with those important to the temple or who had official religious power among the Jewish people; again, Jerusalem was their milieu. This does not mean Jesus discounted his ancestral traditions or rejected the value of Jewish rituals; by no means. But he did not hobnob with priests or others who wielded official, structural authority. Jesus was interested in speaking with and listening to the common people and the destitute, not the socioeconomic elites (most of whom could be expected to reject his message in any case).

Finally, Jesus claimed to speak for God not by virtue of any particular training or educational credentials but because his understanding of God and the divine message was *true*. While Jesus clearly seems to have been immersed in the Scriptures and trained in traditional Jewish ways of interpreting them, he never insisted on that training as validating his message; rather, the truth of the message validated his authority (e.g., Matt 7:28–29). In other words, Jesus presented himself as a prophet, called by God to reveal a message specific to the people of his time and place. He worked outside the typical structures of power and conveyed a message that challenged the rich and powerful. He confronted an ancient version of the "gospel of wealth," repudiating it as an abomination before God. His

1. The Sea of Galilee actually is a freshwater lake. It also goes by the name of Lake Kinneret (i.e., "Harp Lake," due to its shape), Lake of Gennesaret, or Lake Tiberias. Nazareth is about twenty-four miles west of the lake, while Capernaum is right on the lakeshore.

fundamental message called his hearers to "repent," that is, to turn their lives around and return to covenant faithfulness (4:17).

This was not a call to "religious" behavior; Jesus never once spoke of tithes or ritual sacrifice. His message was a revival of the prophets of old: a call to live honestly and justly, treating everyone around oneself with mercy and generosity. Jesus's words and deeds validated each other, and proved that he was a trustworthy guide for those whose hearts were set on life in harmony with the creation and the Creator, the God of Israel. It was a message of hope and peace to a conquered and downtrodden people. While the Matthean community had a different demographic than Jesus's original audience, they still found much to love in his story of justice and hope.

Jesus Calls Disciples (4:18–22)

Unlike the Hebrew prophets, who tended to work alone or with one junior partner (e.g., Elijah and Elisha), Jesus begins by creating a community. The call of disciples highlights a few fishers found plying their nets near the shore of the Sea of Galilee. Notably, the first ones named are two pairs of brothers, one pair apparently rather well off (since their father owned the fishing boat). GMatthew says "immediately" they responded to Jesus's invitation to join his ministry (4:22). This implies that Jesus and his message were already known in the area and had garnered a good reputation, but it also serves as a way of highlighting the charismatic authority God bestowed upon Jesus.

While the individuals named in this scene all are men, Jesus had both women and men disciples. For cultural reasons, the Matthean community does not highlight the women disciples' *public* presence, but they remain central to the group. Indeed, as we will see later, the Matthean scribes recognize that the community would not exist without them. Except for the women disciples of Jesus, there would be no story to tell.

Ministry to the Multitude (4:23–25)

Jesus and his handful of early disciples "went around all of Galilee" (4:23), spreading the message of the coming of God's *basileia*—a pretty ambitious itinerary given that the region of Galilee covers approximately 750 square miles. The point, of course, is not the literal claim that Jesus covered all this territory but that his reputation spread all throughout the region due to his ministry in key towns. It also highlights that Jesus did *not* spend time in Judea during this early ministry. He did not "work the system" to gain a reputation with the religious and political leaders; he stayed among the common folk.

GMatthew says that Jesus taught in the Galilean synagogues, proclaimed the gospel, and cured people of illness and disease. As a result, "his fame spread to all of Syria" (4:24a), the region northeast of Galilee along the Mediterranean coastline, and interested crowds came from several areas in the vicinity, including the predominantly gentile towns of the Decapolis, on the east side of the Jordan River, as well as Jerusalem and other Judean towns. What attracted people from so far away? Would people really travel 125 miles from Jerusalem to Capernaum simply to hear a prophetic preacher call for a return to covenant faithfulness in preparation for the coming reign of God?

Maybe, but GMatthew here highlights not the words of Jesus but his healing ministry: "They brought to him all who were sick with various diseases and racked with pain, those who were possessed, lunatics, and paralytics, and he cured them" (4:24b). That last phrase, "he cured them," provides the key to Jesus's initial popularity. GMark presents this same dynamic, depicting the crowds viewing Jesus as a miracle worker (and thus totally misunderstanding who he really was). GMatthew is not as blunt on this score, but the scribal authors realize that the healing miracles could mislead people into a false understanding of Jesus's true identity and role. Properly understood, the miracles validate Jesus's gospel message; wrongly understood, they lead people to view Jesus as some sort of demigod rather than the fully human Messiah of Israel.

The gospel Jesus preached was one of present salvation—that is, wholeness, health, healing—from the true God who wills the health and wholeness of all creation. The gospel message focused on God, not Jesus; and Jesus's healing miracles showed the truth of that message. However, the miracle-worker focus of the mob detracted from the gospel. The authors of GMatthew know that Jesus's miracles drew people to him, but they also risked totally skewing people's understanding of Jesus and of his divinely appointed message. To head off that kind of misunderstanding of Jesus and the gospel, GMatthew mentions the miraculous healings but immediately shifts to a substantial collection of Jesus's teachings. This way, the focus stays on Jesus's message, not on what the crowds might obtain by associating with him.

The Sermon on the Mount (Matt 5–7)

The first lengthy discourse of Jesus is set on a mountain, with Jesus positioned up above the crowd that has gathered around the base of the hill. Clearly, GMatthew is playing a "new Moses" theme here, as will recur at various points in the Gospel. Unlike Moses, Jesus does not spend forty days alone with God on the top of the mountain; he already spent the forty days in the wilderness after his baptism, so he is fully prepared with the message he's been given to reveal.

The Beatitudes (5:1–12)

Rather than starting with a decalogue of divine commands, Jesus begins with nine statements of divine blessing on particular types of people and behaviors. The first eight of these follow what is called a *macarism* formula, "blessed are the X, for they will receive Y." The ninth one states a blessing and reward without strictly following the *macarism* formula.

The Beatitudes, as they traditionally are called, belong in part to Q material; GLuke presents an earlier, shorter set of Beatitudes with an accompanying set of curses (Luke 6:20–26). Because they are shorter, simpler, and less in conformity with what would have been popular opinion at the time, the Lukan Beatitudes likely represent the text closer to Jesus's actual teaching as remembered in the Q tradition. Comparing the Matthean version with the earlier version reveals important details about the Matthean community and their "spin" on the gospel of Jesus.

> Then he looked up at his disciples and said: Blessed are you who are poor, for yours is the kingdom of God. Blessed are you who are hungry now, for you will be filled. Blessed are you who weep now, for you will laugh. Blessed are you when people hate you and when they exclude you, revile you, and defame you on account of the [Human One]. Rejoice on that day and leap for joy, for surely your reward is great in heaven, for that is how their ancestors treated the prophets. (Luke 6:20–23)[2]

2. The typical translation, "Son of Man," over-masculinizes the underlying Greek phrase (*huios anthropos*), so has been modified to follow what twentieth-century scholars suggested. While *huios* does mean "son," *anthropos* means "human being," not "man" (the Greek for which is *andros*). Functionally, the phrase means "child of the human race," which is cumbersome, to say the least. Hence, the shortened title of "Human One" seems preferable.

> Blessed are *the* poor *in spirit*, for *theirs* is the kingdom of heaven. *Blessed are those who mourn, for they will be comforted. Blessed are the meek, for they will inherit the earth.* Blessed are *those* who hunger *and thirst for righteousness*, for they will be filled. *Blessed are the merciful, for they will receive mercy. Blessed are the pure in heart, for they will see God. Blessed are the peacemakers, for they will be called children of God. Blessed are those who are persecuted for the sake of righteousness, for theirs is the kingdom of heaven.* Blessed are you when people revile you and persecute you and utter all kinds of evil against you falsely because of me. Rejoice and be glad, for your reward is great in heaven, for in the same way they persecuted the prophets who were before you. (Matt 5:3–12)

The quotation from GMatthew includes italics to show the additions to the Q version of the Beatitudes, represented by the quotation from GLuke.

The first detail we notice is the change of address, from "you" in Q to "they/those" in GMatthew. The Matthean community does not identify with the poor, the hungry, the weeping; they know persons who are poor, hungry, and weeping, but "they" are other than the audience of GMatthew. Perhaps as an attempt to overcome the implied remoteness of "those" people, at least in part, the opening beatitude changes "poor" to "poor in spirit." If they have the right attitude toward their resources, even those with wealth can count themselves "poor in spirit."

Another obvious difference is the addition of the beatitudes about the meek, merciful, clean of heart, peacemakers, and those "persecuted for righteousness," and the additional detail that such persecution puts the audience in the company of the earlier Israelite prophets (Matt 5:4, 5, 7, 8, 9, 10, 12). In the aftermath of the great revolt, these blessings upon those who work for peace and justice would provide important and timely encouragement to community members. The elimination of the "woes" section, which was present in Q and is retained in GLuke (Luke 6:24–26), serves the same pacifist purpose.

Memorable Forms of Teaching (5:13–48)

The Beatitudes illustrate one of the key features of Jesus's teaching: It was expressed in ways that are easy to remember. The formulaic structure of each phrase means one need remember only the key words in each set. As we can see from the growth of the first set of three in Q to the eight in GMatthew, it was a simple development to add beatitudes to the list.[3] When the Matthean community added the sayings about the meek, merciful, clean of heart, peacemakers, and those who suffer persecution to uphold justice, they were highlighting different aspects of Jesus's teaching that he had expressed in many other ways. Putting them in these formulaic expressions was a useful teaching tool that helped the audience remember these key aspects of the gospel message.

Jesus used other memorable forms of teaching, including similes and metaphors. The comparisons of those who embrace the gospel as "salt of the earth" and "light of the world" (Matt 5:13–16) pose striking comparisons with everyday realities experienced by the audience. Both salt and light were valuable resources whose presence made life flourish and whose absence caused humans and nature to wither and die. Salt not only preserves perishable items; it prevents dehydration during exceedingly hot summer months. Light is not only necessary for photosynthesis; it makes possible all sorts of human activity that cannot be done safely in darkness. Deeds worthy of emulation are done openly, in the light; so, the natural environment for those who follow the gospel is daylight.

Lest some of the audience members think Jesus's teaching contradicts or abrogates the word of God in the Jewish Scriptures, the Matthean Jesus states explicitly that he totally affirms "the Law and the Prophets," that is, the Bible known to the Jews of his day (Matt 5:17–20). Jesus has come to "fulfill" that received message (v. 17), to bring it to completion, not to overturn it in any way. Among the disciples of Jesus, Torah observance must be greater, not lesser (v. 20).

The next section (Matt 5:21–48), often called "the antitheses," initially seems to contradict this attitude, but a careful reading demonstrates that this surface impression is mistaken. Each section begins, "You have heard it said X"—that is, you have heard this saying when the Torah is proclaimed—"but I tell you Y." The framework seems to imply a rejection of X, but that is never the case. Each conclusion Y constitutes not a rejection of the statement from Torah but rather a heightening of the safeguards around that prohibition or behavioral warning. For example, not only should the audience avoid adultery; they should avoid even *imagining* such an action (vv. 27–28). Extreme measures are recommended to ensure one does not cross the line (vv. 29–30).

3. Yet another set appears in a later noncanonical work called The Acts of Thecla; that one includes thirteen beatitudes.

Rather than a husband being given the right to unilateral divorce for any reason, as long as he legally frees his wife to remarry (v. 31), the husband is denied such univocal power. The assertion that divorce "causes" the wife to commit adultery reflects the economic straits into which a divorced woman was thrown (and often still is). While any dowry was supposed to be restored to the woman upon divorce, that did not necessarily take place, and she had no means of recourse if those resources were not returned to her control. Jesus's ruling restricts traditional patriarchal prerogatives; it rejects the abuse of women through manipulation of divorce laws and repudiates the then-common Greco-Roman practice of a man using a series of marriages, divorces, and new marriages to climb the socioeconomic ladder (as, e.g., notoriously done by Herod the Great and Herod Antipas).

The rejection of oaths (5:33–37) establishes that one should always speak the truth, in every circumstance. If one is known as a trustworthy truth speaker, a vow is irrelevant. Indeed, not speaking the truth is an insult to God, tantamount to a violation of the commandment against bearing false witness.

The section on the *lex talionis* (5:38–41) heightens that restriction as well. The original context for the "law of retaliation" was not to *require* in-kind punishment for a misdeed, but rather to *restrict revenge* to no more than the same damage as originally inflicted (e.g., see Lev 24:20). The Matthean Jesus clearly knows that this was restrictive legislation, and he ups the ante. Retaliation itself is forbidden, or even resisting insult and forced labor. This sometimes has been construed as a doormat policy, so it's important to note the details provided in the examples.

Being struck on the right cheek (v. 39) involves a backhanded slap; in other words, this is an insult as if to a child or slave, not a punch in the face. Facing up to such an insult shames the one who slapped you and prevents you debasing yourself to the same low level.

In the case of the lawsuit (v. 40), handing over your undergarment as well as your cloak publicly shames those who brought the suit; they are shown to be so greedy they caused your public nakedness. Of course, this assumes ancient social mores that valued such virtues as generosity and temperance and disdained such vices as avarice.

Going the extra mile after being impressed into labor (v. 41) is a mode of passive resistance. Roman soldiers were permitted to impress civilians into carrying supplies and material, but for one mile only. Then the individuals had to be released and the soldiers had to look for others to take over the loads. Going an additional mile could get the soldiers into serious trouble with their centurion, and Roman military discipline was nothing if not stringent. Even if the soldiers were not punished as a result of the extra mile, that extra stint changes the whole situation to one of *voluntary* labor; intended victims become active agents.

The last section here (5:43–48) commands a love not only of friends and neighbors but of enemies. In biblical language, "love" is never an emotion or visceral impulse of some sort. Emotions cannot be commanded; attitudes and behaviors can. Love involves an attitude of respect for others and engaging in behaviors for their benefit. Nor is there any "hierarchy of loves" as some recent politicians have claimed. The demand to love even enemies means there is no limit to who *must* be included in the scope of behaviors that build up the human community. The social boundaries that mark friend vs. enemy, neighbor vs. alien, are overthrown. The coming reign of God includes everyone, without exception. Is this easy? No. The divine command is summed up in the final sentence: "So be perfect, just as your heavenly Father is perfect" (v. 48).

Religious Practices: Prayer, Fasting, Almsgiving (6:1–18)

The next section turns to actions commonly considered "religious" practices, although it is worth noting that Jesus makes no categorical distinctions among all the behaviors he teaches. From his perspective, rooted in the biblical tradition, telling the truth and turning the cheek are just as "religious" as prayer or almsgiving.

At least as important as the behaviors encouraged are the attitudes that accompany them. Hypocrisy appears repeatedly as an attitude to avoid (e.g., Matt 6:2, 5, 16). Engaging in prayer, almsgiving, fasting, or any other act related to divine worship must be done "in secret" rather than in front of any audience who might give the person credit for the actions (e.g., Matt 6:4, 6, 17–18). One should pray, give alms, fast, and perform other "righteous deeds" (*mitzvot*) simply because they are right; not for the sake of public honor or any other kind of human reward. This repudiation of public acclaim runs totally counter to common Greco-Roman mores, central to which is *philotimia*, the love of honor. One gains respect and power in a community not by doing acts of benevolence but by being *known* for doing them. The idea of benefactors having someone "blow a trumpet" before them sounds like hyperbole, but it is the kind of behavior associated with civic leaders whose benefactions include public monuments and buildings with engraved inscriptions to tell the world who donated the work.

The audience is enjoined to avoid "babbling" during prayer (vv. 7–8), as if God will not listen to a simple request but must be badgered into action in response to lengthy petitions and repetitions. God is "father" of those who pray, so wants what is best for the petitioner. No repetition is necessary; in fact, God knows in advance what the petitioner needs. A simple request is not showy but more effective in revealing the petitioner's trust in God's goodness and benevolence.

The Lord's Prayer, which follows these general instructions on prayer, provides the model for the simple and effective way to pray. The Matthean version here is longer than the Q original, again mostly preserved in GLuke. It is easy to see this when they are read together. The italics show the likely changes or additions from the original saying of Jesus as preserved in Q.

> So he said to them, "When you pray, say: 'Father, may your name be revered as holy. May your kingdom come. Give us each day our daily bread. And forgive us our *sins*, for we ourselves forgive everyone indebted to us. And do not bring us to the time of trial.'" (Luke 11:2–4)

> This is how you are to pray: "*Our* Father *in heaven*, hallowed be your name, your kingdom come, *your will be done, on earth as in heaven.* Give us today our daily bread; and forgive us our debts, as we forgive our debtors; and do not *subject* us to the final test, *but deliver us from the evil one.*" (Matt 6:9–13)

The Lukan version of the prayer is simpler and shorter, addressing God simply as Abba and not worried about distinguishing this "father" from any other. The version in GMatthew shows the kind of development that would naturally occur in liturgical practice: *our* father is addressed because the speakers are praying in a community rather than in private. The intimate address to God might have seemed presumptuous, equivalent to Dad, so the Matthean community substituted "our father" (*Abbenu*) and added the descriptor "in the heavens" as another way to show respect.

The blessing of the divine name and invocation of the kingdom remains the same across both versions and clearly was an aspect of Jesus's own prayer. Likewise, the request for daily bread; relying upon God for sustenance (e.g., manna in the wilderness [Exod 16]) was characteristic of Israel during the journey from Egypt to the promised land and now is presented as characteristic of the faithful who await the imminent revelation of God's *basileia*. What does that "kingdom" look like? The Matthean community explains it by the additional phrase asking that God's "will be done, on earth as in heaven" (6:10).

The Matthean version of the petition concerning forgiveness is closer to the teaching of Jesus himself. Forgiveness of debts and the plight of the poor form central aspects of Jesus's teaching, and the parallel between our debts and those who are indebted to us is another case of the memorability of the sayings of Jesus. The Lukan community apparently saw the notion of indebtedness to God as counterintuitive—or impossible to overcome, since everything that exists comes from the generosity of God—so this first half of the petition was modified to refer to "sins," offenses against God, rather than debts.

The Matthean community slightly adjusted the petition to be preserved from temptation, fearing that the language of "leading" implied divine culpability, so instead we see a request to be preserved from the ultimate test, with the additional petition to be safeguarded from the evil one (the adversary of God's beloved ones, Satan). The final petition may be inspired by the prayer of Jesus in Gethsemane to "let this cup pass from me" (Matt 26:39); it has the effect of linking the community of disciples with Jesus himself.

Treasures, Light, and Dependence upon God (6:19–34)

The sequence about treasures (6:19–21), light (vv. 22–23), obedience (v. 24), and dependence upon God (vv. 25–34) provides specific details about what it looks like for God's *basileia* to be present already in the lives of the followers of Jesus. This presence has real-life and potentially far-reaching effects within and beyond the community of disciples. This teaching of Jesus directly opposes any attempt to separate religion from economics.

Obedience to the injunction to store up treasures in heaven, rather than in an earthly treasure house, would have immediate economic effects on members of the Matthean community and those in their wider circle. Putting funds in a storehouse takes them out of circulation, which indirectly causes unemployment and a plethora of other economic problems. Putting them into circulation, however, creates jobs, support businesses, provides loans for those who need them, and generally promotes the economy in a number of ways. A community that pools and utilizes their economic resources creates prosperity for everyone—not in an excessive amount for any individual but enough to raise even the poorest among them to a respectable and sustainable standard of living.

This practice, of course, runs totally counter to prevailing economic dynamics, whether in the Greco-Roman world or in our own. Unregulated economies create plutocrats who take more and more funds out of circulation; they manipulate prices, lowering the cost of luxury items while stockpiling basic commodities and thereby inflating those costs. Precisely this dynamic existed in the mid-80s CE when wealthy Roman land- and business owners stockpiled corn and other basic commodities, raising their costs beyond reach for the average person, driving countless persons into debt slavery while flaunting their wealth in conspicuous consumption of luxury goods (Rev 6:6). Jesus's teaching about wealth has clear, concrete implications for the real world here and now. It prepares the believing community for God's *basileia* made manifest in the teaching and practice of Jesus.

The saying about serving either God or money (6:24) reinforces this teaching about treasure and presents it in a pithy, memorable way. Jesus's saying repeats the challenge in Josh 24:15, "Choose today whom you will serve." Everyone in the ancient world knew that there were spiritual powers for good and for evil; one could not live without taking sides. As the famous twentieth-century American folk singer and songwriter Bob Dylan put it, "Gotta Serve Somebody." True allegiance can be given to only one "master," the acquisition of wealth or obedience to God. There is no "gospel of prosperity" here. Wealth is a sign of avarice, not virtue; sin, not blessing.

How does the saying about light/sight fit with this basic theme? It may seem like a non sequitur, but a connection appears in the last phrase focusing on what happens "if the light in you is darkness" (v. 23). Essentially, this saying concerns prejudice. Nearly everyone has met someone who simply refuses to face facts, no matter what. Such individuals may assert that the Earth is flat, climate change is a hoax, a particular race or gender is genetically defective rather than fully human, or any of a hundred other claims that indisputably have been proven false; they are impervious to the evidence. Their "eye is bad" and darkens every experience. Following one's prejudices means not following God, serving darkness rather than serving the light.

What is the "bottom line" of Jesus's teaching about finance? "Seek first the kingdom and [God's] righteousness" (6:33a). When the Matthean community quotes these sayings of Jesus against anxiety, it may seem to present a rather too-rosy picture. If one thinks of the hyper-individualistic economic environment in which many people live, these sayings seem totally impractical. In the context of the earlier teaching regarding treasure, however, this becomes realistic. With the community pooling their economic resources, no one need worry about food, clothing, or shelter.[4] God would provide, not through some miraculous intervention but through the community of those truly seeking divine righteousness.

Judging and Pearls (7:1–6)

The sayings about judgment and pearls are put together to ensure they are not misunderstood. While the followers of Jesus should not be quick to condemn (7:1–5), that does not mean rolling over and playing dead in the face of clear injustice (vv. 5–6). Disciples need to be aware of their own failings and work to overcome them. They can help each other in this endeavor, as long as both parties remember humility.

The "pearls" saying, on the other hand, concerns outsiders, not other disciples; the insulting epithets of "dogs" and "swine" makes that clear.[5] Jesus's followers need to recognize that they cannot change the behavior of outsiders, so they ought not to waste their energies in that direction. Save the pearls of wisdom for those who will listen, the Matthean Jesus says. This language suggests that the Matthean community has had some run-ins with outsiders in their vicinity and that the insider/outsider relationships remain somewhat fraught.

The Power of Prayer, the Golden Rule, the Narrow Gate (7:7–14)

The encouragement to rely upon God in prayer hearkens back to the wilderness period, when everything Israel needed for sustenance—water, bread, meat—came from divine providence. As mentioned with regard to the baptism scene, Jesus's ministry and preaching calls Israel to return to their covenant relationship with God. This imagery regarding the efficacy of prayer reminds the audience of the attitude Israel had toward God during the wilderness honeymoon leading up to their entry into the promised land. At this early point in the Matthean story of Jesus, the "ask and it will be given

4. We see a parallel to this in Acts 4:32–35.

5. While both labels are insulting, the twosome of dogs and swine suggests there are both Jewish opponents (the "dogs") and gentile ones (the "swine").

to you" language may sound a bit rosy, but the Matthean community knows about the miraculous feedings Jesus was remembered to have done (Matt 14:13–21; 15:29–39). They have every reason to believe they can rely upon God to answer prayer and bless their community of disciples.

What often has been called the Golden Rule (7:12) is a positive statement of a common teaching thought to sum up the entire Jewish Bible ("the Law and the Prophets"). Another version of this saying, attributed to Hillel the Elder (who died ca. 10 BCE), frames the teaching in proscriptive language: "What is hateful to you, do not do to your neighbor; that is the entire Torah; the rest is commentary; go learn it."[6] Commentators sometimes debate the relative virtues of the prescriptive versus proscriptive way of framing this teaching. The former encourages initiative while the latter puts the brakes on offensive or hostile behaviors. Either serves as a succinct reminder of the purpose of the Law and the Prophets for shaping correct behavior and building positive relationships within a community and with outsiders.

The saying about the "narrow gate that leads to life" reinforces the importance of following those behavioral rules. God is merciful and rich in blessing for those who are faithful, answering prayer for their basic needs. But that does not give carte blanche to do whatever one chooses or to behave in ways that are destructive of the fabric of the wider community. The Matthean Jesus holds disciples to an exacting standard. There is no cheap grace here.[7]

True Prophets, True Disciples, Solid Foundations (7:15–27)

This final section of the Sermon on the Mount builds on the theme of the narrow gate by warning the community against false prophets or teachers, false disciples, and faulty foundations.

False prophets look tame (sheeplike) but really are dangerous and hostile (wolflike). They are duplicitous, saying one thing but doing another. How does one distinguish between the true and the false teacher or prophet? The Matthean Jesus is not complacent or naïve. He adjures the audience to use empirical evidence to tell whether prophets and teachers are true or

6. Hillel the Elder, quoted in Babylonian Talmud, Šabb. 31a; cited in Glatzer, *Judaic Tradition*, 197.

7. The phrase "cheap grace" was coined by Dietrich Bonhoeffer in ch. 1 of *Cost of Discipleship*, Bonhoeffer's exposition of the Sermon on the Mount.

charlatans. The advice is repeated twice in this passage, which implies that the community has been hurt by false teachers in the past and needs to be wary about being suckered again. "By their fruits you will know them. . . . So by their fruits you will know them" (7:16a, 20).

What about true disciples versus fake ones? A similar standard applies for discernment here. It is wrongheaded to think that those who follow the correct forms of worship are actually true disciples. Discipleship has to do with behavior in the "real" world, not worship. Miracle working and other flamboyant behaviors mean nothing. Only those who do "the will of my Father in heaven" will be counted as true disciples. Since the Matthean Jesus has just used this first sermon to outline that divine will, God's expectations for disciples should be amply clear.

Learning from true teachers and living as true disciples need to be built on solid foundations if the disciples aim to last through the final test. "Everyone, then, who hears these words of mine and acts on them will be like a wise [person] who built [a] house on rock" (7:24). Contrariwise, those who hear but do not do what Jesus teaches are like the fool who built a house on sand. Fierce weather came, "and it collapsed and was completely ruined" (7:27b NABRE). Lip service is empty. Living the teaching is the only thing that matters. Again, the Matthean Jesus is eminently practical, using empirical evidence to discern between those who are true disciples and those who are self-serving hypocrites. There is no leeway for "do as I do but not as I say" attitudes. Only those who walk the walk are reliable, whether teacher or disciple.

End of GMatthew Book 1 (7:28–29)

The Matthean scribes conclude this first compilation of Jesus's teaching with a formulaic ending reminiscent of what is said of Moses toward the conclusion of the Torah:

> When Moses had finished reciting all these words to all Israel, he said to them, "Take to heart all the words that I am giving in witness against you today; give them as a command to your children, so that they may diligently observe all the words of this law." (Deut 32:45–46)

> When Jesus finished these words, the crowds were astonished at his teaching, for he taught them as one having authority and not as their scribes. (Matt 7:28–29)

A similar formula recurs at the conclusion of each of the other four discourses in GMatthew (Matt 11:1; 13:53; 19:1; 26:1), which is one of the reasons scholars have viewed this gospel as framed around five "books of Jesus" similarly to the way the Torah comprises the five books of Moses.

The Matthean text does not state that these words of Jesus are given "in witness against you today," nor that they are words to be given "as a command your children, so that they may diligently observe all the words of this law" (Deut 32:46), but the intertextual hints suggest that the Matthean scribes wanted their audience to hear these overtones in the conclusion of Jesus's first sermon. Instead of repeating those claims about the words of Moses, the scribal authors focused on the impact of Jesus's teaching on his audience. Their "astonishment" matches the awe the witnesses will display at the miracles Jesus will be shown to do in the later parts of the gospel.

In both Jesus's teaching and works, the power and authority of God are revealed. Jesus does not teach with the kind of inherited authority that priests and scribes have, reliant on the pedigree of former priests and scribal teachers. Rather, Jesus has authority like that of the great prophets of Israel who spoke directly with and for God. The comparison with Moses, the greatest of prophets and lawgivers, establishes this point for the predominantly Jewish audience of GMatthew. Yet even gentile converts among the Matthean community could understand this claim of charismatic, divinely given authority as opposed to the kind of traditional credentials that scribes or teachers have. The teaching of Jesus is reliable in a way dramatically different than that of other teachers. If one wants authentically true teaching that reveals the best way of living in relationship with God and God's creation, Jesus is the one to trust.

Conclusions

This first of his discourses in GMatthew presents Jesus as a new Moses figure, teaching from a mountaintop over an extended period of time to a gathering in Galilee but symbolic of all Israel. Jesus is a "greater than Moses" figure; the forty days and nights in that deserted place of temptation (Matt 4:1–11) prepared Jesus for life, not simply for this first discourse that renews the law.

Jesus uses common techniques of Jewish wisdom teaching to convey his good news (gospel) of the coming of God's empire, which will supplant all human governments (including the Roman Empire) and all those who collaborate with such unjust regimes. These teaching strategies include the use of simple metaphors of everyday realities like light and salt and common mnemonic devices like macarisms and antitheses. The audience experiences Jesus's teaching as authoritative, grounded in his very identity, earning conviction beyond what one would grant a trained expert like the scribes or priests.

Jesus's teaching builds on the ancestral traditions of Judaism ("the Law and the Prophets") not "the smallest part of a letter" of which will pass away until the direct rule of God is established—presumably making such divine directions no longer necessary. This "best of all possible worlds" imagined by Jesus and denoted in his teaching as "the *basileia* of God" is already being revealed in the ministry of Jesus and in the lives of his women and men disciples.

Those disciples are not individuals attached to Jesus; Jesus called them to form a *community* of disciples who model the *basileia* in their relationships with each other. This strategy is demonstrated initially by the fact that Jesus invites two sets of brothers (4:18–22). It will become clearer as the gospel story unfolds.

As will become plain as we progress through GMatthew, Jesus expected the culmination of God's coming *basileia* to appear very soon, within the lifetime of his original disciples (Matt 24:34). The Matthean community, writing this gospel two generations later (ca. 80–85 CE), realized that this estimated timeline was overly optimistic. As a result, they expanded on Jesus's teaching to fit their new circumstances and modified some of it to attenuate the discrepancy between what Jesus taught and their current reality (e.g., "blessed are the poor" becomes "blessed are the poor *in spirit*" [Matt 5:3a]). The gospel story continues with this tensive relationship between what Jesus himself taught and what the Matthean community believes Jesus *would* teach if he were present among them in their day.

Review and Discussion Questions

A. Review Questions

1. What are some of the features of GMatthew that present Jesus as a "new Moses" figure?
2. According to GMatthew, what is Jesus's understanding of and relationship to the Jewish Scriptures ("the Law and the Prophets")?

3. Christian tradition, especially in the interpretation of GMatthew, has viewed Jesus as (at least implicitly) founding the church. What elements of GMatthew do you see as supporting this interpretation of Jesus's actions?

4. What are some key features of the *basileia* proclaimed by Jesus?

B. Discussion Questions

1. Why is it important to recognize the Jewishness of Jesus in GMatthew? What difference might it make to contemporary Christian–Jewish relations if Christians foregrounded Jesus's embeddedness in Jewish culture and heritage the way GMatthew does?

2. What significance do you see in Jesus's calling of a community of disciples rather than a number of individuals? How does the discipleship-in-community model challenge the me-and-Jesus dynamic popular in some Christian circles today?

3. Some sectors of contemporary US culture seem to have rejected outright key elements of Jesus's teaching, especially those that have to do with love of neighbor, caring for the poor and downtrodden. What elements of Jesus's teaching and example in GMatthew do you see as confronting that me-centered attitude? What social ethic do you see the Matthean Jesus exemplifying?

Chapter 4

THE MISSION OF JESUS & CO.

The Galilean Ministry (Matt 8:1—11:1)

THIS SECOND "BOOK" WITHIN GMatthew focuses on the ministry of Jesus and companions in Galilee. It leads with a series of healing miracles, which the Matthean scribes use to reinforce the atypical nature of Jesus's authority. Moses was known for a few miracles specifically commanded by God (e.g., water from the rock [Exod 17:1–7]), but the series of miracle stories gathered together in Matt 8–9 depict Jesus as a "greater than Moses" figure. These miracles are done at Jesus's initiative, with which God collaborates. Interspersed with a cluster of healing miracles we find a nature miracle or two and dialogue about what true discipleship entails. The section culminates with the commissioning of "the Twelve" and a discourse about the kinds of demands and dangers disciples will face.

Wonderworks of the *Basileia* (Matt 8–9)

This section of GMatthew has a similar feel to the first few chapters of GMark, which has a series of miracle stories in quick succession. In fact, these miracle stories are taken from GMark, although slightly rearranged. GMatthew intersperses brief teaching elements among the miracles, which gives the audience momentary respites to absorb the significance of Jesus's actions and the power of God revealed in his works. Still, the primary agenda here seems to be to convey the authority of Jesus over illness and the forces of nature.

The Leper Is Made Clean (8:1–4)

The first healing, the "cleansing" of a leper (8:1–4), highlights Jesus's Torah-observant practice: he commands the healed person to "go show yourself to the priest, and offer the gift that Moses prescribed" (v. 4). This would provide testimony to the wider Jewish community about the cured person's status and ability to return to communal worship. It also would affirm Jesus as a healer and lend some institutional authority to his activity.

From the practical point of view, this detail is rather curious. Both in its original placement (Mark 1:40–45) and here, the miracle is situated in Galilee, while any priests would be associated with the temple in Jerusalem, potentially two- or three-weeks' journey south. This suggests that the historical incident took place in Judea rather than in Galilee but has been "relocated" to suit the purposes of the evangelists. The Matthean audience is not likely to have been bothered by this detail; since GMatthew is being composed after the Romans sacked Jerusalem and destroyed the temple, the point is moot.

The Cure of the Centurion's Servant (8:5–13)

The scene shifts from one type of outcast, a Jewish leper, to yet another, the slave of a Roman soldier. The centurion certainly was a gentile; his slave would likely be a captive from a prior military engagement, so there is no way to know whether the person was a Jew or gentile. Regardless, an enslaved Jew in a gentile household would be viewed as debased, so we have two social outcasts here.

The dialogue between Jesus and the centurion focuses on their ability to command. The centurion speaks of his ability to command the soldiers or enslaved persons under his authority. He views Jesus as having similar command authority, although the narrative does not make clear whom or what Jesus would be commanding.[1] Jesus proclaims the centurion a model of "faith" unlike any he has yet found among the Jewish people (8:10). The faith here at least includes the conviction that Jesus will work for the best interests of the centurion's slave—a point that is confirmed in the final verse of this scene. The "let it be done" language (v. 13) fits the common biblical practice of using passive voice to indicate divine action.

1. This story, taken from Q, has a parallel in Luke 7:1–10, but the object of Jesus's command is not clear in that version either.

The narrator makes explicit that this prayer of Jesus is immediately answered: the slave was healed "at that very hour."

Peter's Mother-in-Law Cured of Fever (8:14–15)

The brief vignette that follows initially appears to shift the focus to a more central Jewish audience rather than the "outcasts" of the previous two miracles, but this is a Jewish woman, marginalized by her gender. No one speaks in this scene. Jesus simply enters the house and violates all propriety by touching this fevered woman. The mere touch of his hand relieves her fever. She responds by rising up[2] from her sick bed and "ministering" to Jesus and his companions.

Other Healings (8:16–17)

The narrator tells of a number of other healings that took place "in the evening" (v. 16), after workers would have been released from their labors. The narrative compression here implies that the cures were too numerous to itemize. Instead, we get the two categories of demon possession and physical illness. Jesus healed the sick and exorcised the demonic spirits "by a word" of command, thereby answering at least part of the question raised in the earlier scene with the centurion. The scribal authors of GMatthew take the opportunity to connect Jesus's healing activity with the Isaianic prophecy about God's servant (Isa 53:4).

Potential Disciples (8:18–22)

A narrative aside indicates that by now there was a crowd following Jesus, so he withdraws "to the other side," yet some still pursue him.[3] An interested scribe volunteers to become a disciple. Jesus does not reject his overture but does indicate that his kind of discipleship is different than what the scribe might expect. Unlike the typical teachers of that time, Jesus has no permanent residence to provide the home base for the teacher-disciple relationship. The scribe is welcome to become a disciple of Jesus, but he must be prepared to adopt an itinerant lifestyle to do so (8:20).

2. This language may hint at resurrection imagery.

3. This narrative glitch presumes that Jesus has been teaching along the Sea of Galilee, although GMatthew does not include that geographical detail.

Another potential disciple temporizes, asking Jesus to "let me go first and bury my father" (8:21b). The narrative does not indicate how long a wait this might involve; it is not clear that the man's father is even ailing, much less dead. Jesus's response is more demanding than with the scribe: "Let the dead bury their own dead" (v. 22b). In other words, if you want to be a disciple of Jesus, you must turn your back on your family, now, without delay.

Such "harsh" sayings are atypical for this gospel but not unusual for Q material, which dates to the 40s. In those early days after his earthly mission, the community of disciples thought Jesus would return very soon to establish God's *basileia*. The disciples must be ready to cooperate in that endeavor, at a moment's notice, no matter what it might involve.

Calming the Storm at Sea (8:23–27)

Jesus now shifts location and, illustrating the correct behavior just outlined, disciples follow him—into a boat on the Sea of Galilee. Suddenly the sea, that ancient symbol of chaos, begins to quake and waves swamp the boat, threatening to sink it. Jesus, meanwhile, snoozes unconcerned. Fearful of perishing, his companions awaken Jesus. "Having arisen," he censures the winds and sea, and a "great calm" falls (v. 26 NABRE), replacing the "great storm" (v. 24). All the observers marvel, asking what sort of person can command the obedience of even the wind and sea. This question remains open for now.

The language here intentionally prefigures the final scenes of GMatthew. The images of quaking and rising recur in the discourse about the final judgment (Matt 24:7) and in the scenes of Jesus's death (27:51b–52) and resurrection (28:2). Jesus "arises" in the boat, being awakened from sleep, similar to the way Jesus arises from the sleep of death in the tomb. In other words, this scene is a post-resurrection appearance moved back in time to appear during Jesus's Galilean ministry. In its current placement, the scene serves to hint at the future, when the death and resurrection scenes will provide the final answer to this question of just who Jesus is.

Healing of the Gadarene Demoniacs (8:28–34)

Jesus makes yet another geographical shift, to the east side of Sea of Galilee, an area GMatthew identifies as "the territory of the Gadarenes" (8:28).[4] This area is called the Decapolis, the "ten-city" region. As far as we can tell, Jesus's ministry was largely directed toward the Jewish population of the Roman province of Judea, which included Judea, Samaria, and much of Galilee, Idumea, and Perea. There were Jews in the Decapolis, as synagogue remains illustrate, but the area had a largely gentile population, so it is interesting that Jesus would go there.

The story introduces two people identified as demon possessed. They live near the tombs, which would be situated along the road outside of the town; they are literally the living dead. They continually accost passersby, making the road treacherous. When Jesus comes into view, they challenge him in curious language: "What have you to do with us, Son of God? Have you come here to torment us before the appointed time?" (v. 29 NABRE). The "appointed time" has an apocalyptic flavor and refers to the time when God's *basileia* will finally be established. Even without having heard Jesus preach, the demons are enough in touch with the spiritual world that they recognize Jesus as God's final messenger and inaugurator of God's kingdom.[5]

The next detail we hear concerns a herd of swine (8:3). This provides another indication that we are in gentile territory, since pigs are not kosher (Lev 11:6–7) but were the sacrificial animal of choice among the Romans. The demons plead with Jesus that, if he is going to drive them out of the people, to let them enter the swine instead (8:31). Jesus permits that apparent compromise, yet immediately the swine self-destruct, rushing headlong into the sea and drowning (v. 32). The swineherds tell the tale to the other townsfolk, who come out and appeal to Jesus to leave their region (8:33–34).

This scene is drawn from Mark 5:1–20 but is much abbreviated in the Matthean version. The Markan story has a barely disguised political agenda, depicting the possessed person in shackles and chains, identifying the possessing demon as "Legion" (Mark 5:9), and with the demons begging

4. The Markan original of this story identifies Gerasa instead, but that is unlikely. It was nearly four times as far from the sea as was Gadara.

5. Note that the "Son of God" language does not mean here what it later came to signify in credal statements like that from Nicaea (325 CE). Many figures in the Hebrew Bible are called "Son of God" because they have a special role among God's people (e.g., the king in Pss 2 and 110).

Jesus not to send them out of the region (Mark 5:10). The Matthean scribes, writing in the aftermath of the failed Jewish revolt against Rome, temper the anti-Roman sentiment of the Markan story. They also eliminate the former demoniac's request to become a disciple of Jesus and Jesus's command instead that he should preach to his "family" about "all that the Lord in his pity has done for you" (Mark 5:19). Instead, this one exorcism seems to conclude the Matthean version of Jesus's ministry among the people of the Decapolis and leaves no one behind to speak to the gentiles there about what the God of Israel had done among them.

Healing a Paralytic (9:1–8)

Jesus again crosses the Sea of Galilee, returning to Jewish territory, "to his own town" (9:1), presumably Capernaum.[6] Some people of the town meet him, carrying a person suffering from paralysis. A new theme is introduced here: the forgiveness of sins. Jesus proclaims the sufferer's sins forgiven, which prompts objections from some "scribes" in the audience, who view this as blasphemous. This detail looks like another element from the final portion of the gospel that has been moved forward in the storyline. The temple priests had the right to declare God's forgiveness; that was not viewed as "blasphemy." Jesus did not say "*I* forgive your sins"; he simply affirmed "your sins are forgiven" (9:2c)—again, the passive voice indicating divine action. Jesus is arrogating to himself the right to speak for God, as the priests and prophets did, but this is quite different than claiming to *be* divine. The charge of blasphemy does not fit here, although the evangelists certainly remember it as an accusation against Jesus at the end. Bringing it forward into Jesus's healing ministry implies that the accusation had more to do with jealousy than with the facts about Jesus.

In response to the implicit challenge to his proclamation of the forgiveness of sins, Jesus replies with a counter-challenge: Which is easier, declaring sins forgiven or commanding a paralyzed person to walk (9:5)? This rhetorical question presumes the former is easier, so Jesus does in fact command the person to arise, pick up the stretcher, and go home (9:6b). The person obeys, arousing astonishment in the onlookers, who "glorified God who had given such authority to human beings" (9:8). This

6. This is another story taken from GMark, which does specify Capernaum as the location (Mark 2:1–12). The Matthean version is significantly abbreviated versus the original story and does not require any roof repairs after Jesus is finished.

final detail is worth repeating: This authority has been granted to human beings, plural, not simply to one human being, Jesus. Nor does this—or any other miracle of Jesus—prove that Jesus is anything other than a divinely blessed human being.

The Call of Matthew (9:9–13)

The next "call" scene again shows Jesus crossing boundaries, this one having to do with a rejected group within Judaism. The scene is taken from Mark 2:13–17, where the potential disciple is identified as Levi, son of Alphaeus (Mark 2:14). Here we find the name Matthew, which probably indicates an important person in the history of the community that produced this gospel. In the lists of the Twelve that appear in the Synoptic Gospels and Acts, the name Matthew recurs, whereas no Levi is mentioned (see Matt 10:2–4; Mark 3:16–19; Luke 6:14–16; Acts 1:13). There might have been two different individuals, but we will focus on the case of Matthew, since that is who is named in this gospel.

This individual is identified as a "toll collector," someone who collects customs duties at the gated entrance (the *portorium*) to a city—in this case, Capernaum. His status later is confused when he is classified as a "tax collector" by those who object to Jesus's association with him (Matt 9:16), but these are two distinct roles. A tax collector would go around to business owners rather than be sitting at a toll booth, so the role of toll collector makes better sense in these circumstances. In either case, the person works for the Roman government—specifically, for Herod Antipas, who was tetrarch of this region. His job would be to collect duties from those travelling on the Via Maris that ran through Capernaum, and he might also have been in charge of leasing the fishing rights for the Sea of Galilee.

The vast majority of people in this area would be engaged either in the fishing industry or agriculture, so all would be affected by the customs duties, and the fishers would have to endure leasing costs in addition to the tariffs. We don't know how much money would be involved, but business owners never like taxes of any kind; it is safe to assume that they would view such charges as onerous and inhibitive of trade. In addition, many Jews objected to the Roman presence in the land of Israel, so local government officials tended to be viewed askance. After all, was not the Sea of Galilee part of the land of Israel? Why should the Galileans have to pay to fish on their own lake?

In addition to such ideological objections, there were pragmatic ones. The tax- and toll-collecting positions allowed relatively free rein for graft and other types of corruption. Collection methods tended to benefit local elites and so served to widen socioeconomic inequality, with the proverbial rich getting richer and the poor becoming destitute. In short, few of their Jewish neighbors would be pleased to associate with members of this predatory group.

Jesus breaks the mold here by calling Matthew to join the community of disciples; and Matthew breaks the mold by leaving his job and complying with Jesus's call. In fact, it is in the context of table fellowship that we next see them, the most intimate of social interactions in the ancient world. It is not clear whether the meal takes place at the house of Matthew or Jesus, but the gathering includes "tax collectors and sinners" as well as other men and women disciples of Jesus (Matt 9:10). A group of Pharisees learn of the company Jesus keeps and object to this association, but Jesus asserts that "those who are well do not need a physician, but the sick do" (9:12 NABRE). The Matthean scribes add a quotation from Hos 6:6 to connect this cross-boundary behavior with divine mercy (v. 13a). The section concludes with the rest of the Markan saying, "I have not come to call the righteous but sinners" (v. 13b; Mark 2:17).

Some have asserted that the Pharisaic objection to Jesus's association with sinners has to do with ritual purity, but we have no explicit evidence to support this claim. Ritual purity pertains to temple worship; Jesus is in Galilee, nowhere near the Jerusalem temple. In addition, we have no details about what the "sinners" have done that would make them ritually impure, but Torah amply provides for modes of purification. This is not a case of ritual impurity but rather of social mores.

The gospels depict the Pharisee party as trying to remain aloof from persons who might lead them away from strict observance of the Torah, and "sinners" would do just that. The fact that the Pharisees object to Jesus's behavior suggests some affiliation with them, or at least shared interests. As we saw with the Sermon on the Mount, Jesus's preaching invites his audience to renew their covenant commitment—a perspective that the Pharisees would value and respect. Their strategies differ, however. The Pharisees try to gather the "pure" into a somewhat separatist movement, while Jesus involves himself with all sorts of "riffraff." Both want their followers to come into deeper relationship with the God of Israel, but their strategies and target populations differ dramatically.

Fasting (9:14–17)

A similar question arises in the next scene when Jesus is asked about fasting. In this case, a somewhat more sympathetic group, the disciples of John the Baptist, invite Jesus to explain his non-fasting behavior. Fasting indicates mourning or repentance, but Jesus uses the metaphor of a wedding feast to justify his meal behavior (9:15). Again, this vignette comes from GMark, as do the following wisdom sayings about new versus old patches on a cloak and new versus old wineskins (Matt 9:16–17; Mark 2:21–22).

Although the scene is situated during the ministry of Jesus, it is quite possible that this question arose during the early evangelistic period, when followers of John the Baptist posed some competition for the Jesus movement. The bridegroom imagery fits well with the claim that Jesus inaugurated the reign of God. This image will recur later in some of the parables unique to this gospel.

One of the often-overlooked dynamics of fasting involves its socio-economic class context. Those who are destitute often go without food, but that is hunger, not "fasting." Fasting involves voluntary hunger, whereas destitution involves chronic, involuntary hunger. Those who persistently go hungry cannot afford to fast; when food is available, they must eat or die. There is no telling when another meal will be available. When considering the ministry of the historical Jesus, rather than the Matthean version of him, "fasting" does not fit well with many of the women and men disciples who followed him. The feeding miracles later in the gospel illustrate the importance of sharing food with those who do not have any for themselves. So, it could be that Jesus and the disciples were not known for "fasting" because too many of them came from situations of food insecurity.

Healing Doublet: The Official's Daughter and a Hemorrhaging Woman (9:18–26)

This next section interweaves two healing miracles involving women, one a twelve-year-old maiden and the other an older woman who has suffered from chronic bleeding for those same twelve years.[7] The maiden is from a wealthy family, daughter to one of the leading men of the town.[8] The father

7. Mark 5:26 says the hemorrhaging woman ran through all her resources with doctors, to no avail, but Matthew includes no details about her at all.

8. Mark 5:22 names him Jairus and calls him a "ruler of the synagogue." Whether a ruler of the town or more specifically of the synagogue, the girl's father is a wealthy and influential man in the town.

comes to Jesus, pleading with him to lay hands on the girl and revive her from death.[9] Jesus goes to the father's house, the disciples following along.

Meanwhile, the older woman has no one to plead her cause; she resolves to take matters into her own hands, quite literally, by touching the fringes on Jesus's outer garment (Matt 9:20–21).[10] Jesus turns around, sees her, and speaks to her: "Take heart, daughter; your faith has made you well" (9:22a). The narrator affirms the woman's physical cure (v. 22b), but at least as important is the healing affirmation of Jesus's gaze and speech. For perhaps the first time in twelve years, a Jewish man looks at her directly and sees her, recognizing her importance as a fellow human being. And, for the first time in years, the woman has a family: Jesus speaks to her, calling her "daughter"; all the while, she is standing in the midst of his other women and men disciples, her new sisters and brothers.

The scene shifts back to the maiden's family: Jesus arrives at their home to find funerary musicians and a crowd of mourners making a tumult (v. 23). Jesus commands them all to leave, asserting that the girl is only asleep (v. 24). The crowd mock this claim, but they do exit the premises. Jesus takes the girl's hand and she awakens, rising up (v. 25). The narrator concludes the scene by affirming that the news spread all around.

Contrary to the Markan version of this doublet, the Matthean scribes streamline both elements significantly. Some of the "magical" elements of the original miracles are eliminated: Jesus does not feel the power going out of him when the older woman grabs his *tzitzit* (Mark 5:30a); the group traveling with him is smaller and composed of people already known to Jesus, except for this one interloper, so it takes no effort for Jesus to see who touched his garment; Jesus does not speak any words when calling the maiden back to life. The evangelists seem to be trying to avoid the misapprehension that Jesus was simply a magician. GMark handles that challenge by using the literary device called the "Markan secret," but

9. GMatthew heightens the situation; the original Markan version has her "at the point of death" (Mark 5:23).

10. The *himation* is an outer garment somewhat like a toga but rectangular instead of oval shaped. It is worn over a tunic and can be draped in various ways. The word often is translated "cloak," although the typical size of the *himation*—five yards of fabric—makes a pretty excessive size for a cloak. The text speaks of the woman grabbing not the *himation* itself but the "fringes" on the garment, the *tzitzit* required in Num 15:37–41 and Deut 22:12 as reminders of the wearer's commitment to observe all the commandments of the Torah.

the Matthean scribes apparently thought it more effective simply to omit potentially misleading details.

Healing Two Blind Persons (9:27–31)

In motion again, Jesus is accosted by two persons with sight impairments, who address him with the messianic title of "Son of David" and beg for him to take pity on them (9:27). Jesus enters an unidentified house, and they follow him there. Jesus confronts them directly: "Do you believe that I can do this?" They respond, "Yes, sir!" (AT).[11] Jesus touches their eyes, utters the prayer, "According to your faith, let it be done to you" (v. 29), and their sight was restored—literally, "their eyes were opened" (v. 30a), implying that they also came to a new understanding of Jesus's identity. Atypically for GMatthew, Jesus warns them not to tell anyone (v. 30b)—a command they promptly disobey, publishing their news abroad (v. 31).[12]

Healing a Mute Person (9:32–34)

In the next scene, an unidentified group bring a demon-possessed mute person to Jesus for healing. Jesus casts out the demon, which frees the person to speak. The crowds are amazed at what they witness, but a sour note is introduced at the end of the scene. "The Pharisees" start to pass a detracting rumor: "By the ruler of the demons he casts out the demons" (9:34). This miracle and succeeding accusation come from Q (Luke 11:14–15), although the original version does not blame any particular group for originating the rumor. The Matthean community apparently had a negative history with the Pharisee party, and that antagonism affects their narrative about Jesus.

11. The word *kyrios* means "sir," "lord," or "master." Most biblical translations use "Lord" here on the principle that the blind persons are affirming their faith in Jesus. The question concerns his ability, not his identity, so I have left the translation more neutral.

12. This command of silence (and disobedience) may simply be a carryover from GMark, which uses this literary device of the "Markan secret" to warn the audience against misunderstanding Jesus as merely a miracle worker. As a literary device, it functions fairly well. On a pragmatic level, however, the prohibition makes no sense. The family, friends, and neighbors of the blind persons certainly would notice and be excited about the change in their condition. And *rumor volat*, especially in small towns and villages where virtually everyone knows everyone else. GMatthew tends to avoid presenting Jesus as prohibiting reports of his miracles because it makes the teacher par excellence look somewhat a fool when his command is ignored.

The Compassion of Jesus (9:35–38)

This series of miracle stories ends with a sweeping survey of Jesus traveling all through the region, to various towns and villages, teaching in the synagogues, "proclaiming the gospel of the *basileia*, and curing every disease and illness" (v. 35 AT). Jesus is remembered as being moved with compassion (literally, "gut feeling") for the crowds, who were troubled and dispersed,[13] "like sheep without a shepherd" (v. 36c). Jesus invites the disciples to pray that God will send more workers for the "harvest" (9:37–38), which segues into the next section where Jesus takes the initiative in this regard.

The Mission Discourse

The Mission of the Twelve (10:1–15)

GMatthew speaks of "the Twelve" for the first time in this scene, providing a list of names that parallel those that appear in GMark (Mark 3:16–19), although in a slightly different order. Unlike in the earlier gospel, GMatthew includes no "call" narrative designating this group; the audience is expected to know who they are. GMatthew here equates "the Twelve" with "the disciples"—a rhetorically effective but historically false move. The Twelve represent all Israel, the "twelve tribes," so commissioning them to assist Jesus in spreading the gospel symbolically enlists the aid of all Israel in the Jesus movement. Unfortunately, once the primary audience of GMatthew went beyond the Jewish world, readers no longer viewed themselves as members of the people of Israel; thus, many interpreters of GMatthew erroneously have construed this group as exclusive rather than inclusive, as if Jesus had only twelve disciples, all male. Evidence throughout the remainder of the canonical gospels demonstrates that this is a false reconstruction of the Jesus movement, but it is a difficult reflex for readers to overcome. It is important to keep reminding ourselves that the group of women and men disciples of Jesus was much larger than these twelve named individuals.

Jesus is depicted as delegating authority to "the Twelve"—again, to all believing Israel, represented by this group—to cure every disease and cast out demonic spirits (Matt 10:1). He also commissions them to preach the gospel "to the lost sheep of the house of Israel" (10:6), that is, to proclaim

13. The term here hints at the diaspora, which is the present situation of the Jewish people when GMatthew is being written.

that "the *basileia* of heaven is at hand" (10:7 AT). They are not to go to gentiles or Samaritans at this point (10:5). Nor are they to take any resources with them, not even a walking stick for modest protection (10:9–10). Nor are they permitted to accept any payment (10:8b); their work is freely given, demonstrating the free gift of God. While their mission is conceived as an itinerant ministry, an element of stability is included: Once arriving in a particular town, the emissaries should find a household to host them and stay there until their work is completed (10:11). The blessing of divine peace, shalom, will rest on the worthy but not on the unworthy (10:12–13). Any place where they receive no welcome should be symbolically shamed, with an implicit threat of future destruction: The departing emissaries are told to shake the dust from their feet as they leave the town (10:14–15).

The itinerant ministry envisioned here seems to fit an early period of evangelism, perhaps during Jesus's own lifetime but certainly soon thereafter. Q scholars tend to identify this dynamic with the Q community, that is, the group that first gathered the Q sayings materials into a composite source. The itinerant ministry model has the benefit of spreading the gospel over a wide area in a relatively short period of time. The key drawback is that it is not sustainable over the long haul. Later in GMatthew, we will see an implicit recognition of this fact when the model of ministry changes. The more obvious evidence of the change, however, is the very existence of this gospel. Itinerant groups simply do not have the resources to collect the Jesus traditions, research their connections with earlier Jewish ones (including those in the Bible), and create this narrative of Jesus's life and ministry.

Coming Persecutions (10:16–33)

The emissaries of Jesus are cautioned about how they might be received by particular audiences they will encounter. Thus far in the narrative, Jesus has been accepted pretty readily by most groups; the Gadarenes' request that Jesus leave their region (8:34) and the rumor mentioned after the cure of the speech-impaired person (9:34) are the few cases to the contrary. This preparatory speech, however, warns the missionaries against expecting a positive reception. The language of being "handed over" to town councils, synagogue, governors, and kings, especially with the mention of a gentile audience (v. 18), reflects a conflicted period well after the time of Jesus himself. The book of Acts details this scenario, using Peter and Paul as exemplars, but GMatthew simply presents the warning. The only individual in the gospel who is "handed over" in like manner is Jesus himself (27:2 and passim). Similarly, the internecine struggles mentioned (v. 21) reflect a time closer to that of the Jewish revolt rather than the lifetime of Jesus or immediately afterwards.

The disciples are encouraged to flee persecution, when possible (v. 23), but also to trust to divine inspiration when haled before the courts (10:19–20). In a flash-forward to the trial and execution of Jesus, his followers are warned not to expect better treatment than Jesus himself received (10:24–25). The slander about Beelzebul is heightened here: Jesus is not merely in collusion with the prince of demons; he is identified as the demonic prince himself (v. 25), and his followers can expect to be charged with similar demonic associations.

These potential charges, however, are not to be feared. The disciples should be bold, preaching freely what Jesus taught, for the truth will out (10:26–27). The only appropriate fear is that toward God, who will reward or punish as appropriate (v. 28). God watches over the beloved; even the hairs on their heads are counted (v. 30). This section concludes with the Q saying that Jesus will "acknowledge before my Father in heaven" all those who recognize him and deny those who deny him (10:32–33; Luke 12:8–9). As long as one is faithful, there is naught to fear.

Jesus: A Cause of Division (10:34–36)

The next few verses repeat the warning that Jesus will be a cause of division within families: "I have come to bring not peace but the sword" (v. 34). The younger generation (son, daughter, daughter-in-law) will oppose their elders (father, mother, mother-in-law) on the question of loyalty to Jesus. Again, such statements fit better with the situation during the First Jewish Revolt than they do during the lifetime of Jesus himself. The Matthean community has lived through such turmoil and includes these kinds of details when reflecting upon the sayings of Jesus himself.

Conditions and Rewards of Discipleship (10:37–42)

For the first time in GMatthew, we hear explicit mention of willingness to face potential crucifixion ("to take up the cross") as a condition of discipleship (10:38). Family cannot take priority over following Jesus (v. 37)—a totally countercultural demand, whether for Jewish or Roman society. Only those who are willing to put their lives on the line are truly worthy of Jesus (v. 39). Much of this material is taken from Q, which was written in the period leading up to the Jewish revolts, when such extreme demands fit the social environment (Luke 14:25–33).

On the positive side, anyone who accepts one of the disciples of Jesus will be rewarded as if they did that action for Jesus himself. The followers of Jesus represent him, so they receive both injuries and benefactions on his behalf (Matt 10:40–42). God will reward them as their behaviors deserve. This brief warning of rewards and punishments hints at the longer "final judgment" scene expounded toward the end of the gospel (25:31–46).

End of GMatthew Book 2 (11:1)

The section concludes with the now-familiar formula, "When Jesus had finished giving these commands" (11:1 NABRE). This editorial marker indicates the end of the second book of the New Torah of Jesus. The concluding note to this section is harsher than the first one, a sign of more difficult choices to come for Jesus and his followers.

Conclusions

This second "book" in GMatthew broadens Jesus's ministry to include a wider population of recipients of his message, partly through the way Jesus himself crosses sociocultural boundaries and partly by the way Jesus recruits emissaries (the Twelve) to assist him in spreading the good news of the coming reign of God. The rewards of association with Jesus are made clear in the results of his healing miracles, including the psychological healings represented by the exorcisms. The final discourse in ch. 10, however, also highlights the challenges of discipleship, including the potential loss of one's family and even one's life. GMatthew now broaches the willingness to "take up the cross" to follow Jesus. Disciples need to face the fact that they may be executed in the same ignominious way as happened to their teacher. Yet the rewards of faithfulness are great; true disciples will be affirmed before the throne of God by Jesus himself.

Review and Discussion Questions

A. Review Questions

1. What kinds of wonderworks does GMatthew depict Jesus doing?
2. Who do the Twelve represent in GMatthew? Why "the Twelve" rather than "the Seven" or "the Twenty" or some other number?
3. Many contemporary Christians seem to have forgotten that Jesus spoke in rather harsh terms about the cost of discipleship. How do Jesus's example and teaching of the *basileia* challenge the so-called "gospel of wealth" that is being preached today?

B. Discussion Questions

1. What significance do you see in the wonderworks GMatthew depicts Jesus doing? Which of these miracles do you find most significant to you personally? How so?
2. Jesus recruited emissaries to help spread the gospel of the *basileia*. How do contemporary Christians continue to fulfill that role?
3. Why do you think GMatthew has Jesus expressing the cost of discipleship in such stark terms? Have there been times in your life (or in the lives of those close to you) when you have experienced those costs for yourself? How do you handle those moments?

Chapter 5

TEACHING IN PARABLES

(Matt 11:2—13:53)

THIS THIRD "BOOK" OF Jesus in GMatthew focuses on Jesus's spreading fame, the question of his true identity and divinely established role, and his use of parables and metaphors to spread the good news of the coming *basileia* of God. Most of the material is drawn from GMark; the remainder derives from Q, with parallels in GLuke.

Jesus and John

Messengers from John the Baptist (11:2–6)

The section opens with an inquiry from John the Baptist, who has been held in prison by Herod Antipas during the entire time of Jesus's public ministry thus far (see Matt 4:12). John had a number of disciples who remained at large and apparently suffered no negative repercussions from visiting John in prison. They bring Jesus an inquiry from their master: "Are you the one who is to come, or are we to wait for another?" (11:3). "The one who is to come" refers to the long-awaited messiah who will rescue Israel from foreign domination and restore the Davidic kingdom. The details of that expectation will be disputed later in the narrative, but the immediate response deflects attention from a direct political confrontation. Instead, GMatthew depicts Jesus's reply as focusing on the physical and economic aspects of God's salvific work: "The blind receive their sight, the lame walk, those with a skin disease are cleansed, the deaf hear, the dead are raised, and the poor have good news brought to them" (11:5).

Jesus Testifies About John the Baptist (11:7–15)

Prompted by this inquiry from the baptist's disciples, GMatthew then has Jesus "put John in his place" by speaking of the value of his ministry and message. John is a prophet, and more. The scribal evangelists use Mal 3:1 and Exod 23:20 to argue that John is the forerunner to the messiah, the precursor of the one who will bring in the new and final age but not the messiah himself. To contemporary readers, this seems a moot point, but it was a pressing issue for the Matthean community.[1] John the Baptist was viewed as a messianic figure, and we continue to hear of followers of the baptist movement well into the second century CE.[2] Later in GMatthew, we will hear that Herod Antipas viewed Jesus as John "raised from the dead," hence the great works Jesus did (Matt 14:2). The Matthean community, of course, disagrees with this assessment, but its potency is revealed in the fact that the Matthean scribes judged it necessary to refute the claim.

This section about John is drawn from Q, but the Matthean scribes make special efforts to refute any idea that John the Baptist was the messiah. The Matthean Jesus speaks positively of John but puts him a step down not only to Jesus but to all of Jesus's followers: "Truly I tell you, among those born of women no one has arisen greater than John the Baptist, yet the least in the kingdom of heaven is greater than he" (11:11). John is an Elijah figure (11:14), a prophet speaking God's truth to his generation, but not the messiah. As we saw in the baptism scene (3:14–15), John's role and status are clearly made secondary to that of Jesus, and it remains unclear whether John is included among those who belong to "the kingdom of heaven."

1. For more on this topic, see Culpepper and Anderson, *John and Judaism*, esp. the chapters by Loader ("Tensions in Soteriology") and Culpepper ("Matthew and John").

2. The Mandaeans, as they are now called, still exist today in the Middle East, esp. Iran, Syria, and Jordan. A relatively small religious group, they are estimated to number about sixty thousand. For more information, see Buckley, *Mandaeans*.

Responses to Jesus

Reproaches to This Generation (11:16–24)

The edge of tension returns in the critiques leveled against "this generation." The people are castigated for their wishy-washy responses to both Jesus and John. Nothing pleases them. They complained formerly about John fasting and now about Jesus feasting (11:18–19). The accusation that Jesus is "a glutton and a drunkard" sounds hyperbolic, but slander works best when based on exaggerated facts or partial truths rather than totally concocted from scratch. The proverb "wisdom is vindicated by her works" functions like the assurance "by their fruits you shall know them." In other words, look at the empirical results of Jesus's mission if you want to judge its—and his—value.

The cities of Chorazin and Bethsaida, within easy walking distance of Jesus's home in Capernaum, are singled out for negative attention. Jesus did many "mighty deeds" in those towns, yet the people there did not accept his message (11:20). The tirade alleges that the gentile cities of Tyre and Sidon would have repented immediately if they had experienced anything like the works Jesus did in these Jewish towns. Even Capernaum is made a target of the critique. While these reproaches comprise Q material, dating from the 40s–50s, their placement in GMatthew might reflect some remaining negative feelings concerning the townsfolk's response during the Jewish revolt of 66–73 CE.

Praise of the Father (11:25–27)

A brief prayerful interlude shifts gears in this section. Jesus thanks God for revealing the "secret" of the *basileia* only to the childlike, not to those who are viewed as wise or learned (11:25). GLuke presents Jesus as engaged in prayer on a regular basis, but this vignette of Jesus praying is relatively rare for GMatthew. It appears as public speech—Jesus is said to speak "in reply" to an unnamed person or group—which of course runs counter to the prior teaching about praying "in secret" (Matt 6:6). The remarks function rhetorically as another implicit critique of those who object to Jesus's teaching and ministry and an affirmation of those who accept the Matthean community's claim that Jesus is the one to whom God has "handed over" the entire creation (the prerogative of the firstborn son and heir). So far, we are in the realm of messianic theology, but then GMatthew takes it a step further. Using language similar to that found later in GJohn, the scribal evangelists claim: "No one knows the Son except the Father, and no one knows the Father except the Son and anyone to whom the Son chooses to reveal him" (11:27b; compare John 17, esp. vv. 25–26). This is not merely "like father, like son" language. In the context of the apocalyptic theology of Jesus's proclamation of the coming *basileia*, this functions as revelatory language: anyone who wishes to know God must approach God through Jesus, the sole mediator.

Easy Yoke of Christ (11:28–30)

Is it hard to become a disciple of Jesus? The extensive critiques just reviewed would suggest a resounding yes answer. Perhaps that is why GMatthew rearranges the Q material to put this "yoke" saying here. The invitation to accept the yoke of Jesus draws a comparison with the yoke of the Torah, but understood through the Jesus tradition rather than through Mosaic tradition or other lines of interpretation. The Matthean scribes build on Ben Sirach's invitation to learn wisdom and submit to her yoke (Sir 51:23–26) so as to find "rest" (Jer 6:16) for the weary heart. Rather than multiplying requirements of Torah, Jesus simplifies them, going to the heart of God's commands. This yoke is "easy" because it fits the bearer (unlike a "hard" yoke that is not customized to fit the specific animal who wears it). Yoked in tandem with Jesus, no disciple is left to carry the burden of covenant observance alone; it becomes "light."

Jesus and the Sabbath

At this point, the scribal evangelists return to their Markan source for their gospel traditions. They modify the material from GMark slightly to suit the sensitivities of their more sophisticated audience. Two scenes raise the question of appropriate behavior on the Sabbath, while the remaining material concerns Jesus's identity and the urgency of his message.

Sabbath Harvest (12:1–8)

Jesus and company are walking through a field of grain, plucking and eating kernels as they pass through the field. "The Pharisees" are presented as the opponents here because of the focus on Sabbath observance.[3] Unlike the original story (Mark 2:23–28), the disciples are not "making a road" (Mark 2:23), and the Matthean narrator specifies that the disciples were hungry (Matt 12:1b). Saving human life always takes precedence over any Sabbath prohibitions, so this detail provides an ample excuse for the disciples' behavior without portraying Jesus as abrogating Sabbath regulations.

Jesus is depicted as justifying the disciples' behavior by adducing a rather obscure example of David and his companions eating the forbidden showbread (Matt 12:3–4) and a reference to priestly work required on the Sabbath (see Lev 24:8; Num 28:9–10). This is precisely the kind of argument one might expect from scribes who want to persuade a group focused on Torah interpretation as a centerpiece of their way of life. The punch line, the claim that "the human person is lord of the Sabbath" (Matt 12:8 AT), usually is read in reference to Jesus himself, but the quotation from Hos 6:6 (in v. 7) contradicts such a reading. The Hosea quote has to do with justice for the poor taking priority over ritual observance; and the individuals being defended are the disciples, not Jesus himself.

Sabbath Cure (12:9–14)

The next scene with the Sabbath healing takes place in "their" synagogue (12:9)—a hint that the Matthean community and their opponents maintained distinct worship spaces. Jesus is challenged: "Is it lawful to cure on the Sabbath?" (12:10). There would be no disagreement about an affirmative answer if the person were in danger of death. The question here revolves around someone who is ill or disabled but not in extremis.[4]

The Matthean Jesus makes an argument *ad maiorem*, using the example of rescuing a sheep from a pit (v. 11). If they would judge it lawful to lift the sheep to safety, in spite of the Sabbath prohibition about carrying burdens, then by extension it is permitted to heal a human being, who is inestimably more valuable than the sheep (v. 12). The fallacious element of the argument, of course, lies in the fact that the human being's health is not precarious; a sheep in a pit, whereas not necessarily in imminent

3. The story highlights the fact that Jesus and his companions were harvesting the grain (which is prohibited on Shabbat), but in fact their travel very well may violate the Sabbath laws as well, since there also is a limit to the number of steps one may take on Shabbat.

4. The Markan version of this (Mark 3:4) has Jesus ask, "Is it lawful to do good or to do harm on the Sabbath, to save life or to kill?"

danger of death, still could drown or be killed by predatory animals if not rescued. Nevertheless, the argument follows typical rabbinic modes of interpretation, and Jesus here shows his respect for both Torah and common Jewish interpretive strategies.

The predictable conclusion of the scene is that Jesus does cure the person's disabled hand (v. 13) rather than waiting until the next day. The perhaps less predictable response is that his opponents—here identified again exclusively as "the Pharisees"—"went out and conspired against [Jesus], how to destroy him" (v. 14). The conspiracy exceeds a reasonable reaction to Jesus's behavior at this point in the story, but the evangelists have to compress a significant period of time into the gospel narrative. Iconographic scenes like this one end up being given more significance than they originally would have had.

Jesus as True Messiah

This next section brings to the fore the question of what it means for Jesus to be the true Messiah of Israel.

Jesus as Chosen Servant (12:15–21)

Learning of the plot against him, Jesus withdraws from the area, although crowds follow him and "he cured all of them" (v. 15). Jesus warns the people not to reveal his presence (v. 16). This time, the "secret" seems to be kept. The scribal evangelists use an extensive quotation from Isaiah (42:1–4) to construe this prohibition as evidence that Jesus truly is the "servant of Yahweh" foretold by the prophet.

Jesus and Beelzebul (12:22–32)

The confrontation with Beelzebul, the "prince of demons," has been some time coming. The two earlier incidents in which Jesus is accused of being in league with Beelzebul (Matt 9:34; 10:25) are brought to a head here. The scene ups the ante by depicting one individual as afflicted by demonic possession as well as being blind and mute. The person symbolically represents all those who oppose Jesus, who refuse to see who he truly sees or to speak the truth about him. When Jesus cures all these ailments, the crowd wonders whether he is the "Son of David," that is, the anticipated messiah-king

(v. 23). On the other hand, once again we are told that "the Pharisees" object to Jesus, claiming he uses demonic power to do these miracles.

Contemporary readers tend to view this dispute as a power struggle between the "bad" Pharisees and the "good" believers, with the foregone conclusion that the Pharisees were wrong in their assertions about Jesus. This, of course, is precisely the interpretation the Matthean community wants the audience to make, and they have slanted the narrative to convey that reading. However, it is a grossly unfair presentation of the Pharisee party, who are not likely to have posed strong opposition to Jesus himself. In fact, Jesus's teaching was closer to that of the Pharisees than to any of the other known groups within Judaism of the time. The antipathy reflects conditions less like those between Jesus and the Pharisee than between the Matthean community at the end of the first century and other forms of Judaism in the postwar era.

Nevertheless, the suggestion that Jesus might wield demonic power to do miracles makes perfect sense within a first-century mindset. Miracle working demonstrates spiritual power, but there are good spirits and evil spirits; theoretically either type of spirit could work wonders. In other words, the ability to work miracles does not prove anything about the miracle worker nor about the type of spirit involved. One must use discernment to determine which type of spirit is active. Jesus asserts that one should judge this by the fruits of the actions—a reasonable enough guideline and one that will be reiterated in the next vignette.

The Matthean scribes view Jesus's healing miracles and exorcisms as signs of divine power at work. Jesus cannot be doing exorcisms by demonic power because it is illogical to think of demons striving against each other; it would mean Satan was "divided against himself" (v. 26). GMatthew challenges Jesus's opponents to identify the spiritual power behind their own exorcists, for the same question could be raised about them as about Jesus (v. 27).

The real crux of the matter, however, is what will happen if the opponents admit that Jesus has access to divine power to do these miracles. If so, they will have to admit that his proclamation of the *basileia* is true (12:28). Jesus equates the exorcisms to "tying up the strong man" before plundering his house (v. 29), implying that his audience was living under the thrall of demonic forces that had to be expelled to make way for the reign of God. Miracles in themselves remain ambiguous; however, the good fruits of Jesus's miracles prove that his *basileia* message truly is

God's word and the final age of divine justice has begun to be revealed in the world. Those who deny the divine origins of the gospel commit the unforgivable sin of blasphemy, attributing to Satan what is actually the work of the Spirit of God (12:30–31).

Fruits of the Tree (12:33–37)

The saying about a tree and its fruits continues the argument that one should judge the goodness or evil of Jesus's ministry based on the empirical evidence of its fruits. Do the healings and exorcisms have good results or bad ones? If they have good results, those must derive from divine action, and Jesus and his message must also be divinely sanctioned. Those who would speak on the matter should take care, for they will be called to account for their words at the final judgment.

Demand for a Sign (12:38–42)

The demand for an indisputable sign of Jesus's divine authority is another element of the Q tradition, inserted here in the series of challenges and responses by Jesus. This last challenge is framed as coming from "some of the scribes and Pharisees" (v. 38), groups who would have been interested in Jesus's ministry and would sincerely have been trying to discern whether he was the long-awaited Messiah. GMatthew presents them in a negative light, revealing more about the Matthean community's conflict with them in the 70s and 80s than any antipathy toward the historical person of Jesus.

The challengers are rebuked for implying they have no other evidence on which to judge Jesus's veracity or goodness. In an explicit reference to the resurrection, the "sign of Jonah" is named as the one incontrovertible indication of divine support for Jesus and his ministry (12:39–40). The Jonah reference brings forth the example of Nineveh, the Assyrian capital whose people repented immediately upon Jonah's preaching; even the cows wore sackcloth (Jon 3:6–9)! This gentile people did not require signs and wonders from Jonah; they heard the prophet's word and acted in response. Those who do not heed the word of Jesus should beware lest they end up being condemned by these foreigners who believed God's word without requiring signs.[5] Here we find a hint of the mixed nature of the Matthean community, which includes believing gentiles as well as Jews.

5. Again, there is an interesting flavor of GJohn here (see John 20:29).

Unclean Spirits (12:43–45)

This brief statement about unclean spirits symbolically warns against starting with Jesus and then reversing course and rejecting him. Someone liberated from demonic spirits needs to remain vigilant lest the demonic possession return with even more vengeance than before. The apocalyptic flavor of this warning hints at more explicit sayings that appear in the last discourse in Matt 24–25 (e.g., 24:42).

Jesus's True Family (12:46–50)

In contrast to the one possessed by unclean spirits are the members of Jesus's true family: those who hear the word of God and do it (12:50). Jesus's family of origin does not have first claim on him, nor should this be the case for any of his women and men disciples (10:37). GMatthew omits the scenario in Mark 3:21 where the reason for Jesus's family of origin seeking him is to interfere with his ministry because they think, "He has gone out of his mind." The Matthean community has a more positive view of Jesus's mother and siblings so do not want to present them as opposed to his mission.

Commentators have noted that there are no "fathers" listed among the fictive kinship relations in Jesus's "true" family. Fathers in the Greco-Roman world have total authority over the members of their household; the paterfamilias can kill slaves and chastise his wife and children with no legal recourse on the part of those under his authority. The disciples of Jesus are not to have that kind of relationship with each other. They must be willing to leave their parents behind if those parents do not join as disciples of Jesus (i.e., "let the dead bury their own dead" [Matt 8:22]). The disciples may be mother and siblings to each other, but they have only one Father, God (23:9).

Teaching in Allegories and Parables

The "parable discourse" rounds out this third "book" of Jesus's teaching in GMatthew. This section of the gospel includes allegories as well as parables, and the scribal evangelists seem not to have differentiated between the two forms of oral teaching. The key difference between a parable and an allegory is that a parable has one key point, whereas the allegory functions like two stories overlaid on each other, with multiple points of connection. We get the word *parabola* from the same Greek root as parable, and a parable has that kind of narrative arc with one object lesson aimed to strike the audience right between the eyes. If the parable does not make the audience upset and angry, they are missing the point. Allegories do not have that kind of rhetorical edge. Perhaps that is why the Matthean scribes prefer allegories and even turn some of Jesus's parables into allegories by providing allegorical interpretations of them (e.g., the sower and the weeds).

Parable of the Sower (13:1–9)

A boat along the seashore may seem an odd setting for a parable having to do with farming, but then the farmer in the parable is pretty odd, to say the least. Either this farmer is so wealthy he does not have to worry about wasting seed, or he is a careless idiot. The sower does nothing to prepare the soil or even to focus where the seed is spread. He broadcasts it on good soil and bad, among rocks and brambles, even on the footpath. Such a waste of seed surely would anger needy farmers in Jesus's audience. Anyone with sufficient resources to waste seed like this should share those resources with the poor, hardworking farmers who actually know how to grow crops.

The parable concludes with a miraculous result: the seed that landed in the good soil produced a tremendous harvest of hundred, sixty, or thirty times what was planted. A reasonably good harvest would provide a tenfold yield, so this result from such flagrantly irresponsible behavior would shock the audience. What kind of seed is that? How do we get some?

Inciting that impulse to want the seed is the key point of this parable. Jesus's teaching is meant to move the audience to new behaviors, inspiring the desire to seek and find what God has in store for them—not, in this case, a miraculous GMO seed, but the mystery of the coming *basileia*.

Parables and Discipleship (13:10–17)

GMatthew presents a kinder version of the disciples' behavior than does the earlier gospel from which this parable is drawn. GMark portrays the disciples as dense, not understanding Jesus's parables and needing a "cheat sheet" to figure out what they mean. The Matthean scribes modify this by having the disciples ask why Jesus treats outsiders differently: "Why do you speak *to them* in parables?" (Matt 13:10b). Jesus's rather counterintuitive response is "to you it has been given to know the secrets of the kingdom of heaven, but to them it has not been given" (v. 11). This implies that the parables are intended to *prevent* the audience understanding them.

The Synoptic Gospels present this as the result of Jesus speaking in parables (e.g., Mark 4:10–13; Luke 8:9–10), and parables do require attention to get their point, but presumably Jesus actually did want the audience to understand what he was saying. The apparent fact that many either did not understand or, if they understood, did not want to accept what Jesus claimed, is presented by the Matthean scribes as a fulfillment of the prophecy of Isa 6:9–10. The end result is that only disciples can truly understand the parables of Jesus because such wisdom comes from God to those whose hearts are open. Disciples are truly blessed because they see and hear and understand what remains obscure for outsiders.

Allegory of the Sower (13:18–23)

The "explanation" of the parable of the sower actually is an allegorical interpretation, which takes each element of the parable and equates it with something else. It is as if the interpreters have taken a second story (Jesus's preaching of the *basileia*) and overlaid it on the parable at a slight angle. Thus, each element of the agricultural story becomes a different audience response to Jesus's preaching. We end up with a moralizing allegory that tells the audience how they *should* respond and provides grounds for them to dismiss as fainthearted or avaricious those who do not accept the gospel. Whereas the parable was designed to inspire action, the allegory prompts moral judgment and condemnation of outsiders.

Such allegorical interpretations represent the early church preaching tradition rather than Jesus himself. The Matthean scribes did not invent this interpretive practice; they adopt this particular interpretation virtually unchanged from Mark 4:14–20. Given the conflicted environment in which GMark was written, with the Jewish revolt under way and antagonistic relationships feeding violence both among Jews and between Jews and their gentile neighbors, such a tendency to condemnation of those who are "not one of us," however regrettable, makes sense.

Weeds Among Wheat (13:24–30)

The next story, which is unique to GMatthew, posits a situation in which an enemy sabotages a field by planting weeds among the wheat. When the weeds sprout, the field hands ask the estate owner whether they should pull them up. The "lord" (*kyrios*) temporizes: "Let both of them grow together until the harvest" (13:30a). Then both the wheat and weeds will be gathered, the wheat into the barn and the weeds to burn.

This tale fits the Hebrew category of *mashal* (a thought problem), so often is called a parable, although it doesn't have the single arc we previously identified as the key feature of parables. The typical reading of this *mashal* is allegorical: The wheat plants represent true disciples while the weeds represent false ones. But it is not the job of true disciples to weed the field.

Augustine of Hippo (354–430 CE) provided probably the most well-known interpretation of this story, identifying the field as the church and adjuring overly zealous believers to avoid trying to uproot the tares.[6] It is not yet time for the harvest.

> Let those who are wheat persevere until the harvest; let those who are weeds change themselves into wheat. This, you see is the difference between people and real ears of wheat and real weeds, because with those things growing in a field whatever is wheat is wheat, and whatever are weeds are weeds. But in the Lord's field, which is the Church, what used to be grain sometimes changes into weeds, and what used to be weeds sometimes change into grain; and nobody knows what's going to happen tomorrow.[7]

Whether one chooses to follow Augustine on this interpretation or simply the more general message of waiting for the harvest (i.e., the final judgment), this unique Matthean *mashal* tells the audience to suspend action and let God decide who is a true or false disciple. Putting this story immediately after the allegorical interpretation of the sower has the effect of cooling the condemnation of those who appear to be to be "bad seed."

Mustard and Yeast (13:31–33)

These two parables involve someone embedding an object in a field or a container of flour. The parables do not specify whether the person planting the mustard actually owns the field nor whether it is the woman's own bushel of flour, so it is quite possible these are acts of sabotage. Mustard is an invasive species, so the Talmud restricts how much can be planted and

6. E.g., Augustine, "Sermon 47," esp. §§6, 16–18.

7. Augustine, "Sermon 73A," 295.

where.[8] While some sort of leaven is necessary to make bread, yeast has a consistently negative connotation in Jewish tradition (e.g., Matt 16:6). Both yeast and mustard infiltrate the medium in which they are planted or hidden. The unbridled growth of both elements—mustard or yeast—is the basic point of both comparisons. Once it has begun, there is no stopping the reign of God.

A brief word on terminology may be in order. The mustard seed parable is taken from Mark 4:30–34, and the yeast parable is from Q (Luke 13:20–21). As is the case with the earlier parables of the sower and others, the original version of each of these two parables begins with the phrase "the reign of God is like . . ." GMatthew typically changes this "God" language to "the heavens," substituting a reference to God's dwelling place to avoid the use of the divine name. Many English translations read "the kingdom of heaven" (even though the original is plural), which conveys the unfortunate impression that the *basileia* Jesus proclaimed is an "afterlife" concept that has nothing to do with the earth. The reign of God Jesus preached certainly does have to do with present, earthly existence, as the miracles demonstrate. Contemporary readers need to recognize this tendency to "spiritualize" the *basileia* message and work to counteract that impulse.

The Use of Parables (13:34–35)

This brief section reiterates what was stated in Matt 13:10–15 about Jesus speaking in parables, only with a twist. In the earlier passage, the impact of the parables was to *prevent* the crowd understanding Jesus's message. Here, "the prophet" (actually Ps 78:2) is quoted as predicting the use of parables to *reveal* wisdom. Whether the audience will understand this wisdom teaching remains unspecified.

Allegory of the Weeds Among Wheat (13:36–43)

After these interludes on mustard, yeast, and the use of parables, the Matthean scribes return to the parable of the weeds among the wheat and provide an allegorical interpretation of it. Similar to the interpretation of the parable of the sower, this allegorical reading provides an alternate story line with point-by-point substitutions for the original details. The subtle apocalyptic imagery of the "harvest" becomes fully explicated. "The harvest

8. E.g., Tosefta Seb. 2:9 and Mishnah Kil. 2:9.

is the end of the age, and the reapers are angels" (v. 39), who will gather the weeds/evildoers and "throw them into the fiery furnace" (v. 42 NABRE). Then God's *basileia* will be fully established on earth: "Then the righteous will shine like the sun in the kingdom of their Father" (v. 43a).

Treasure, Pearl, and Net (13:44–50)

The parables of the treasure and pearl follow a consistent "find, sell, buy" dynamic. Someone finds a hidden treasure/valuable pearl and sells everything to buy the treasure field/pearl. The key point of these two parables is to inspire the audience to jump at the chance for the treasure/pearl and sell everything to obtain it; allegorically, it images the call of Jesus to leave everything to follow him and thereby find the treasure of the *basileia.*

The fishnet reiterates the point of the weeds among the wheat allegory. The dragnet pulls in fish of all kinds, which are then sorted, the good to be kept and the bad to be thrown away (13:47–48). The punch line of this parable is almost identical to that of the weeds allegory: "So it will be at the end of the age. The angels will come out and separate the evil from the righteous and throw them into the furnace of fire" (13:49–50a).

These two sets of parables emphasize the reward of following Jesus and welcoming the *basileia*, while warning of dire punishment for refusing to embrace the reign of God.

Treasures New and Old (13:51–52)

Unlike GMark, which presents the disciples as dense and clueless, GMatthew portrays the disciples as understanding Jesus's message—therefore, implicitly, as trustworthy witnesses (13:51). Jesus encourages them to cherish both their ancient traditions and the new revelation God is making known: "Every scribe who has become a disciple in the kingdom of heaven is like the master of a household who brings out of his treasure what is new and what is old" (v. 52). This ideal is clearly what the Matthean scribes are trying to model in GMatthew.

End of GMatthew Book 3 (13:53)

This third book of Jesus concludes with a formula similar to what we have seen in the earlier two books: "When Jesus finished these parables, he left that place" (v. 53).

Conclusions

This third book of Jesus in GMatthew focuses more attention on the choice that must be made either to become a disciple or to reject Jesus and his message of the *basileia*. Jesus is an inspired prophetic teacher, like Moses, yet greater than Moses. Indeed, Jesus is the true Messiah, and John the Baptist was his forerunner—not his competitor. The section begins with a series of miracle stories showing the in-breaking of the reign of God through the work of Jesus and concludes with a series of parables that highlight the choice to be made to cooperate with the reign of God or to refuse. The *basileia* is coming, unstoppable as mustard growing in a cultivated field or yeast leavening flour; the only question is whether to recognize it as the treasure it truly is or to reject it and lose everything at the final harvest.

Review and Discussion Questions

A. Review Questions

1. According to GMatthew, what was the relationship between Jesus and John the Baptist? How does the Matthean Jesus's testimony about John correct the understanding the audience might have gained from reading the earlier depiction in GMark?
2. How does GMatthew modify the story about the Sabbath harvest (Matt 12:1–8) to show Jesus and the disciples as more Torah-observant? Why is that important for the Matthean community?
3. According to GMatthew, how should one judge whether Jesus is truly the long-awaited Messiah of Israel?
4. What is the key difference between a parable and an allegory?

B. Discussion Questions

1. Christian tradition has tended to forget that Jesus himself was a Torah-observant Jew, from the cradle to the grave. Many Christians grow up thinking of Jesus as one of themselves (e.g., a Baptist; a Presbyterian) and are startled to realize that this could not possibly be correct. What are some of the reasons it might be important to remember that Jesus was Jewish? Are there any drawbacks to this?

2. Jesus claimed that his contemporaries could judge whether he truly was the Messiah by looking at the fruits of his ministry. Should the faithfulness of contemporary Christians be judged on the same basis? Why or why not?

3. The Matthean scribes seem to have preferred allegories to parables and basically turned some of Jesus's parables into allegories by providing allegorical interpretations of them. How do parables engage the audience differently than allegories? What do you see as the costs and benefits of the two forms?

Chapter 6

ESTABLISHING THE CHURCH

(Matt 13:54—18:35)

Opposition at Home

Rejection at Nazareth (13:54–58)

THIS NEXT SECTION OF the gospel begins with a scene of Jesus's rejection in his hometown of Nazareth. The locals are unwilling to accept that one of their own, someone with such a modest background, could be a wisdom teacher who speaks with prophetic authority and does wonderworks with the power of God. The Matthean scribes soften the Markan version of this episode, saying Jesus *did* not (rather than *could* not [Mark 6:5]) do many miracles there because of their unbelief (Matt 13:58).

Herod Antipas and John the Baptist (14:1–12)

In somewhat of a delayed reaction, we find that Herod Antipas, the Roman-appointed tetrarch of Galilee and Perea, has heard about Jesus and thinks he is John the Baptist redivivus. Only then do we discover that John is dead. What follows is a story of the most grotesque dinner party ever. Herod had imprisoned John for criticizing his marriage to Herodias, his divorced sister-in-law, which violated the Levitical laws concerning consanguinity in marriage (see Lev 18:16; 20:21). Antipas knew the people regarded John as a prophet, so he arrested John but did not have him executed for fear of reprisals.[1]

While John languished in prison, Antipas threw himself a birthday party at which we are told his stepdaughter performed a dance to entertain the guests—an outrageous claim designed to show the decadence of Herod's court (14:3–6). Herod promised the girl an extravagant reward; prompted by her mother, she requests John's head on a platter (14:7–9). John duly beheaded, the platter is delivered to the daughter, who then presents the head to her mother (14:10–11).

The original Markan narrative is designed to make Herodias look like the one at fault for John's death. The Matthean version attenuates much of that, streamlining the story to the bare minimum of details. The Matthean community knows that Herod executed John, but they are not concerned about the palace intrigue and petty politics of the reign of Antipas half a century earlier. The key point remains that Antipas had John beheaded—and Jesus was alive to hear about it from John's disciples after they buried their master (14:12).

Miracles Among the Jews

The Feeding of the Multitude (14:13–21)

Hard on the heels of the monstrous Herodian dinner party is the miraculous feeding of a vast crowd of five thousand families. The textual location invites the audience to read the two "meals" in light of each other, the one showing the grotesque inhumanity of the Herodian house and the other showing the unstinting generosity of God. The latter shows what the reign of God is and will be like: no one goes hungry, no one is beheaded, and there is no symbolic cannibalism.

The narrator says that Jesus took a boat and withdrew to a deserted place alone, but a crowd followed him around the coast and gathered where he disembarked (14:13). Although his plans for "downtime" were frustrated, Jesus had compassion toward the crowd and cured the sick among them (v. 14). When evening drew on, the disciples reminded Jesus that the place was deserted and encouraged him to send the crowd away so they could go to the villages to buy food. If the area was as deserted as the narrator has

1. This is a modification from the Markan version of the story, which presents Herod himself as viewing John as a righteous and holy man (Mark 6:17–29, esp. v. 20).

said, twice, the likelihood of there being villages nearby with food to sell seems highly unlikely. But we are not to find out.

Jesus's response to the disciples' suggestion is curt, an implicit reprimand for their callous disregard of the needs of these people for whom Jesus himself had compassion: "You yourselves give them something to eat" (v. 16 AT). They object, "We have only five loaves and two fish!" (v. 17 AT). Jesus has the crowd be seated, takes the loaves and fishes, offers the prescribed blessing, breaks them, and gives the pieces to the disciples to share with the crowd. Wondrously, "all ate and were filled" (v. 20)—a condition that might have been a first experience for many of those present. The leftovers filled twelve wicker baskets; the number fed included five thousand households.

The twelve baskets here clearly represent the whole people of Israel (the twelve tribes). Jesus feeds the multitude in a "deserted place" like God fed the Israelites with manna in the desert. The disciples are used as intermediaries to distribute the food, but the food itself comes not from them but from the bounty of God. This is what the *basileia* looks like: The hungry are fed, not sent away to fend for themselves.

Walking on Water (14:22–33)

The scene of Jesus walking on the water follows the Markan story (see Mark 6:45–52) with the addition of some material concerning Simon Peter, taken from GMatthew's special source (M). "Immediately" after the feeding miracle, Jesus commands the disciples to go ahead of him by boat "to the other side" of the lake while he dismisses the crowd and then goes up "the mountain" to pray alone (Matt 14:22–23).[2] As evening draws on, the disciples' boat is still many *stadia* from the shore.[3] Buffeted by the wind and waves, the boat is in danger of swamping. The narrator sets the time as the "fourth watch of the night" (three to six a.m.).[4] This period just before

2. The hill named here probably is what is known today as Har HaOsher, the Mount of Beatitudes, although it hardly constitutes a "mountain." The hill is only 200 meters (approximately 650 feet) above the level of the Sea of Galilee, and actually has a negative elevation of 25 meters (82 feet) below sea level. The mountain image, already in the Markan story, provides another tip of the hat to Moses.

3. A *stadion* is about 210 yards, so "many" *stadia* could be anywhere beyond a third of a mile—certainly too far to row back to shore without swamping in tumultuous seas.

4. Mark 6:46b–47a mentions that Jesus was alone on shore, watching the disciples' boat, and saw that it was being tossed by the waves while the disciples vainly tried to row.

dawn has significant resonances with other miraculous events in the Bible, so the audience is expecting something marvelous—and they are not disappointed.[5] We hear that the terrified disciples see Jesus walking toward them on the sea. Thinking him a phantasm, they cry out; Jesus responds: "Take heart, it is I; do not be afraid" (14:27). Again, the injunction to "fear not" resonates with other biblical theophanies,[6] while the phrase "it is I" (*ego eimi*) repeats God's self-revelation to Moses in Exod 3:15. In short, this brief combination evokes the divine presence come to save.

At this point of Jesus's self-revelation, the Markan story ends—Jesus gets into the boat, the sea calms, and the clueless disciples literally go nuts (Mark 6:51–52)—but the Matthean scribes do not like this rather ignominious ending for the story. They add a unique interlude with Simon Peter: "Sir, if it really is you, command me to come to you on the water" (Matt 14:28 AT).[7] So, Jesus calls him (thereby confirming he is not a phantasm). Simon gets out of the boat and starts across the water toward Jesus (v. 29). But the wind grows strong and fear overtakes Simon; starting to submerge, he calls to Jesus to save him (v. 30). "Immediately," Jesus reaches down and saves him from drowning, although he reprimands Simon for his "little faith" (v. 31). They get into the boat and the wind ceases (v. 32), returning to the original Markan story. Instead of GMark's critique of the dense disciples, the Matthean story concludes by highlighting the disciples' insight: "And those in the boat worshiped him, saying, 'Truly you are the Son of God'" (14:33).

This prompts Jesus to come to them. GMatthew provides no such prompt, implying that Jesus just knows what the disciples need.

5. E.g., Jacob's wrestling for a divine blessing in Gen 32:22–31 occurs during the last watch of the night, as does Israel's liberation from the pursuing Egyptians in Exod 14:25–26 during the exodus event. The most significant parallel to this scene in GMatthew is the resurrection scene "at daybreak" (28:1).

6. E.g., Exod 14:13; Deut 31:6; Josh 1:9; Isa 41:10.

7. The English translations universally translate *kyrie* here as "Lord" (with the capital letter), rather than "sir" or "lord," prejudging Simon's statement and making it look like an affirmation of Jesus's identity, but the sentence itself—"*if* it is really you" (my emphasis)—contradicts this idea. Simon Peter does not know the identity of this apparition, but a polite form of address seems imperative. Who would want to anger a phantasm? Nor does Simon really trust his "lord" once Jesus calls him out onto the water; hence, he sinks and has to be rescued yet again. This dynamic fits well with Simon Peter's conflicted behavior later in the gospel, especially during Jesus's arrest, trial, and the aftermath of those traumatic events.

Several features of this story indicate that it is another post-resurrection appearance that, following GMark, has been relocated to a point earlier in the gospel narrative. Key among those features is the disciples' initial impression that they are seeing a phantasm. The disciples' terror at the ghostly apparition and Jesus's voice telling them to "fear not" both are features of post-resurrection appearances. The *ego eimi* formula fits the believers' post-resurrection understanding of Jesus, as do the worship behavior and profession of Jesus as God's Son. At this location in the gospel narrative, the story serves again to heighten the difference between insiders and outsiders, believers and opponents of Jesus.

Healings at Gennesaret (14:34–36)

A brief vignette ensues in Gennesaret, where the boat reaches landfall. People from all around bring their sick for Jesus to heal. Like the woman with the hemorrhage (9:20–22), all they wanted was to touch the fringes on Jesus's *himation*, and "all who touched it were healed" (14:36).

Interestingly, the text specifies that the *men* of that area *sent out* the word of Jesus's presence to the countryside and *led to Jesus* the sick to be healed. The evangelistic undertones of this version make it clear that the Matthean scribes are overlaying events in Jesus's life and ministry with post-resurrection realities.

Debating the Ancestral Traditions (15:1–20)

Some scribes and Pharisees came to Jesus from Jerusalem to inquire about his perspective on "the traditions of the elders" (i.e., interpretations of the law of Moses). The question is not an informational inquiry but a challenge: "Why do you break the traditions?" (Matt 15:2). Jesus does not interpret the commandments the way they do, so they accuse him of violating the law. This is somewhat disguised in the dialogue to make it look like the issue concerns divine commands rather than human traditions, but the Pharisees were talking about the divine commands *as understood in their tradition of interpretation.*

Rather than arguing with his challengers, Jesus levies a countercharge: "And why do you break the commandment of God for the sake of your tradition?" (Matt 15:3). Jesus quotes the Decalogue command to "honor your father and your mother" (Exod 20:12; Deut 5:16) and asserts that his opponents use the practice of corban (dedication to the temple) in a way that violates the commandment (Matt 15:4–6). We actually have no evidence that this accusation was true; in fact, the later rabbinic tradition agrees with Jesus on the primacy of care for parents over such oaths.[8] The dispute implies that the Matthean scribes were aware of a contemporary discussion of the question, but the "scribes and Pharisees" in this narrative exchange are constructed characters rather than historical ones.

The dispute scene gives the Matthean scribes the opportunity to charge their contemporary opponents with hypocrisy. Building off of Isa 29:13, they assert that their opponents privilege human customs over divine precepts. No doubt the opponents would make the same accusation of the Matthean scribes for privileging the teaching of Jesus, but of course the Matthean community views Jesus's teaching as coming from God, not human tradition.

The scene then segues to Jesus teaching a crowd, where he focuses on the inward requirements of the law and the intention one has when obeying the commandments. The disciples report that "the Pharisees" took offense at what Jesus taught, but in fact Pharisaic teaching agreed with this stance. So, while we have accurate teaching from Jesus here, the Matthean portrayal of the Pharisees is not reliable. Unfortunately, that disparity between rhetoric and history will only get worse as we go along in the gospel narrative.

Miracles Among the Gentiles

Cure of the Canaanite Woman's Daughter (15:21–28)

The narrator shifts scene and relates that Jesus withdrew "to the district of Tyre and Sidon" (15:21)—a rather remarkable claim since Tyre, the closer town, is fifty miles northeast of Capernaum, and Sidon is another twenty-five miles further north along the Mediterranean coast. If Jesus wanted to be alone, this "withdrawal" was a rather extravagant way to achieve solitude—and we quickly discover it did not have that effect.

A woman from thereabouts comes to Jesus to ask him to cure her daughter, who is tormented by a demon (v. 22). GMatthew identifies her as a "Canaanite," using the name of the ancient enemy of Israel, rather than GMark's labels of "Greek" and "Syrophoenician," which simply name her as a gentile from that geographical location (Mark 7:26). The woman

8. E.g., Mishnah Ned. 3:1 and 9:1, from ca. 200 CE.

names Jesus as "lord" (*kyrie*) and "Son of David" (Matt 15:22), titles that honor him in ways he has not experienced before this incident. However, the fact that she speaks first would be taken as an insult, especially since she is a gentile.

Jesus first ignores her plea for help, and the disciples encourage him to send her away (v. 23). He rebuffs her: "I was sent only to the lost sheep of the house of Israel" (v. 24).[9] Still she persists in her pleas, bowing down before him (v. 25). Finally, Jesus rebukes her in rude and racist language, calling her a "dog" (v. 26).[10] In the honor-shame dynamics of the first-century Roman world, this kind of name-calling would function to reestablish Jesus's honor and precedence over the woman. The audience would expect her to cringe away, metaphorical tail between her legs. Instead, the woman makes a startling riposte, which accepts the epithet and turns it on its head: "Yes, Lord, yet even the dogs eat the scraps that fall from their masters' table" (15:27). This response brings Jesus up short, and he finally sees this woman as an equal worthy of attention. He affirms her "faith" and prays that God will do what she has asked. The narrator confirms that in fact her daughter was healed that very hour (v. 28).

In the context of GMatthew, this miracle story involving a gentile woman conveys Jesus's initial reluctance to include non-Israelites in his mission, a reluctance Jesus overcomes because of this interaction with this persistent mother. This scene serves as a watershed not only in that respect, but also because it is the only time he is bested in an argument. A mere gentile—and a woman at that—gets Jesus to change his mind.

Healing the Many (15:29–31)

The narrative teleports us back by the Sea of Galilee and we find Jesus "up the mountain," with "great crowds" coming to him there with "the lame, the blind, the maimed, the mute, and many others" to be cured (v. 30). The crowd was "thunderstruck" when they saw all these people healed: the lame walking, the blind seeing, the mute speaking, and the deformed restored to wholeness (v. 31; compare Isa 35:5–6). The Matthean scribes

9. This rather begs the question of why then he has traveled so far beyond Israel, to this region. The statement serves to set up the distinction between Jesus's own mission (to Israel) and the later mission of the disciples (to the wider world).

10. This was a common term of derision apparently used by both Jews and gentiles for the other group.

present this complex of miracles to show that Jesus fulfills the prophecy of the messianic age.[11]

Feeding the Multitude (15:32–39)

This miraculous feeding of the four thousand households is a doublet of the previous feeding of the five thousand households (Matt 14:13–21), with a few details modified. Jesus takes the initiative, commenting on the crowd's hunger after three days with him on the mountain (v. 32). The disciples present Jesus with seven loaves this time and a few fish. He blesses and breaks them, the disciples distribute the pieces to the crowd, and again all eat and are satisfied. When the leftovers are collected, they fill seven baskets. Because of the numerical symbolism, this feeding is often understood as involving gentiles and therefore paralleling the earlier feeding of the Jewish crowd.

Conflict with the Opposition

Demand for a Sign (16:1–4)

This episode depicting "the Pharisees and Sadducees" coming to Jesus and demanding a sign essentially repeats the episode with "the scribes and the Pharisees" in Matt 12:38–42. Jesus's remarks (16:2–3) about the opponents' ability to predict the weather but not "the signs of the times" typically appear in square brackets in Bible translations. Those square brackets mean the text is uncertain, that is, we do not know if it actually belongs in GMatthew because it does not appear in all of the ancient copies of the gospel. In this case, the two verses serve no real purpose other than insulting Jesus's opponents. Verse 4, which includes the refusal of any sign except "the sign of Jonah," is sufficient to convey Jesus's rejection of their demand.

Given that the passage simply provides a synopsis of the earlier rejection of a demand for a sign, it is interesting to note that "the Sadducees" have been substituted for "the scribes" among the opponents of Jesus. The Sadducee party tended to be prominent in Judea, not Galilee. They disagreed with the Pharisees on multiple points of theology: They

11. Compare to the Qumran traditions, which hold that the Messiah will not only release the captives and comfort the afflicted of the community (11QMelchizedek) but will also give sight to the blind, heal the wounded, resurrect the dead, and feed the hungry (see 4Q521, a.k.a. Messianic Apocalypse).

rejected the Prophets and Writings as important for law and doctrine; they did not believe in the resurrection of the just, nor did they expect a messiah, since neither topic is present in the Torah. It is not clear why the Pharisees and Sadducees are said to approach Jesus together, since the two groups were divided by a number of points of contention. Most likely, the Matthean scribes have replicated the earlier scene and substituted "the Sadducees" for "the scribes" to show that opposition to Jesus was amping up and spreading beyond Galilee.

Leaven of the Pharisees and Sadducees (16:5–12)

Jesus's remarks about the "leaven" of these two groups (v. 6) warns the disciples to avoid the teaching of the Pharisees and Sadducees (v. 12). No details are provided (other than a somewhat amusing case of the disciples being dense and needing their misunderstanding corrected), so apparently no particular theological debates were in view here. Note that "leaven" is used in a highly charged, negative way. It is viewed as dangerous, insidious. This tension seems to reveal more about the Matthean community at the time the gospel is being written than it does about the life and ministry of Jesus himself.

Faith and Discipleship

The next few vignettes address faith and discipleship and thereby balance the negativity of the previous two pericopes that depict conflict with Jesus's opponents.

Simon Peter's Confession (16:13–20)

The "confession" of Simon Peter is perhaps one of the most famous portions of GMatthew and has played an overblown role in Catholic–Protestant debates, with Catholics focusing on Simon Peter, the individual, and Protestants focusing on the content of Simon Peter's affirmation. Because of this conflicted history of interpretation, it is difficult to go back to what the Matthean community was trying to convey here, which probably had little to do with either of these "sides" of the later theological debate.

The scene begins by situating Jesus in Caesarea Philippi, in the tetrarchy of Herod Philip II (rather than Herod Antipas), about twenty-five miles north of Capernaum. Contemporary Banias, it is situated at a natural spring that comprises one of the headwaters to the Jordan River. This city was Philip's capital, and that political location might have inspired Jesus's question "Who do people say that the Human One is?" (v. 13). The underlying version in Mark 8:27–30 has Jesus ask, "Who do people say that I am?" (v. 27), but the Matthean scribes have modified the question to highlight the fact that the question really concerns the identity of the true Messiah, the one God is sending to establish God's *basileia* and end the other political powers.

GMark does not have to consider followers of John the Baptist as messiah, but the Matthean community does. So, of course, the first response to Jesus's question is John the Baptist; Elijah and one of the other prophets are less popular alternatives. Since the Matthean scribes know that none of those answers can be correct—after all, Jesus is the true Messiah—they return to the Markan tradition to ask, "But who do you say that I am?" (Mark 8:29a; Matt 16:15). In the Markan version (8:29b–30), Peter affirms that Jesus is the true Messiah, and that is the end of the discussion; Jesus simply charges them to say nothing to anyone. The Matthean scribes significantly expand this affirmation, starting with a "Hebrew parallelism" that says the same thing twice in slightly different words: "You are the Messiah, the Son of the living God" (Matt 16:16).

Jesus affirms Simon for speaking the divinely revealed truth (v. 17) and then goes on to make a play on words: "You are *Petros* and on this *petra* I will build my community" (v. 18 AT). Much has been made of the "rock" image for Peter, but keep in mind that *petra* does not refer to a great rock or *lithos*. This is not the Rock of Gibraltar here but a little rock or even stony ground. Like in the parable of the mustard seed, the terminology emphasizes the small beginnings of this community Jesus is establishing. In spite of those small foundations, the community will be strong, undefeatable: "The gates of Hades shall not prevail against it" (v. 18b).

The Matthean Jesus gives to Peter "the keys to the *basileia*" (AT), with the earthly power to bind (or compel) and loose, and the affirmation that those decisions will be honored "in the heavens," that is, by God, when the *basileia* is finally established (v. 19). Some have argued that the "power of the keys" was given to the church as a whole, not to Peter alone, but the singular "you" and the second-person singular verb forms all indicate that Peter is being addressed here. Peter does symbolize the entire Jesus community, but he is the initial object of these assurances. These details again imply that the Matthean scribes are reading back into the story of Jesus elements of their own history that took place after the resurrection event.

The episode concludes with Jesus charging the disciples to tell no one he is the Messiah (16:20), which then leads into the passion prediction to explicate what that claim means.

First Prediction of Jesus's Passion (16:21–23)

This first prediction of the kind of death Jesus will suffer, put into Jesus's mouth by the Matthean scribes, mostly follows the earlier version in Mark 8:31–33. In both gospels, the point is to correct the false understanding of the role of Messiah as one leading to earthly glory and political triumph. The language of "from that time on" (v. 21a) marks a shift in the gospel narrative to one that now points toward Jesus's death in Jerusalem. Following GMark, the narrative says Jesus will "undergo great suffering at the hands of the elders and chief priests and scribes and be killed" (v. 21b). The Matthean scribes modify the last part of the prediction to highlight the divine action in the resurrection: "And on the third day [Jesus will] *be raised*" (v. 21c).

Peter's rebuke of Jesus (again taken from Mark 8:32–33) puts in the mouth of this one disciple the natural response of virtually all Jews of the time of Jesus. Nothing in the Jewish Scriptures would have prepared them to anticipate a messiah who would be opposed by the Jewish leaders and executed by occupying gentile forces in Jerusalem. Everything in the tradition would have led them to think that the messiah would be like King Cyrus, who liberated the Jews from the occupying Babylonian forces. Peter's objection to the passion prediction is characterized as the voice of Satan (Matt 16:23), the tempter who would prevent Jesus living up to God's hidden plan for the Messiah. The story serves to "make the case" for Jesus as the true Messiah by presenting this dramatic exchange in which the Matthean scribes correct traditional messianic expectations and replace them with their post-resurrection understanding, now placed in the mouth of Jesus himself.[12]

12. Jesus had to have known he was starting to incur the wrath of some powerful opponents and, as a former disciple of John the Baptist, he clearly knew that death could be the result of such opposition, but the details of this passion prediction—and the later ones—clearly are influenced by the community's post-resurrection perspective.

Conditions of Discipleship (16:24–28)

The ensuing remarks about the conditions of discipleship, again following the earlier version in GMark, highlight the necessity to "deny" oneself to follow Jesus. One must be willing to undergo even crucifixion, like Jesus himself did. Those who are willing to lose their lives for the sake of the gospel will actually find life, while those who continue in opposition to the gospel will end up losing their lives instead. Thus far, the saying repeats the earlier statement in Matt 10:38–39. It then continues with an eschatological warning about the final judgment at the parousia, that is, the glorious coming of the Messiah (the "Human One") with the angels and divine power to "repay everyone according to their conduct" (v. 27).

The Matthean scribes then add an authentic saying of Jesus: "Truly I tell you, there are some standing here who will not taste death until they see the Human One coming in his kingdom" (16:28 AT). Jesus meant this to refer to the parousia, but that did not take place during the timeline Jesus proposed. In fact, GMatthew is being written during the third generation after the life of Jesus, which makes the saying somewhat embarrassing; Jesus was mistaken. The Matthean scribes probably reinterpret the saying as referring instead to the resurrection.

Prefiguring the End

The Transfiguration (17:1–8)

The transfiguration scene is another post-resurrection appearance moved forward in the gospel narrative. It serves to balance off the prediction of Jesus's passion with a positive vision proving that his death will not be the end of everything he has worked to achieve. As is the case with other biblical theophanies, the transfiguration is set on a mountain. The narrator says it took place "after six days" (v. 1), which makes this the seventh day, a Sabbath fulfillment-of-creation image. Jesus takes only three disciples with him to the mountaintop: Peter, James, and John.[13] We see traditional theophany imagery: Jesus's "face shone like the sun and his clothes became white as light" (Matt 17:2; compare Exod 34:29–35; Dan 7:9; 10:6). Next to Jesus appear Moses, the lawgiver, and Elijah, the prophet who will return to usher in the final days. These two greats of Israelite history were

13. The same threesome will be isolated for special attention in the Gethsemane scene during the passion narrative (Matt 26:37).

"conversing" with Jesus, showing that all of their ancestral traditions are fulfilled in Jesus.

Peter, ever eager but not terribly perceptive, seems to identify this with Sukkoth and offers to set up three tents, one each for Jesus, Moses, and Elijah (v. 4). Peter assumes this mountaintop stay will last for some time (perhaps the seven days of the festival). Mark 9:6 points out Peter's faux pas and attributes it to terror, but the Matthean scribes simply pass over the remark, literally overshadowing it with a cloud (v. 5).

Repeating elements of the baptism story, a heavenly voice declares, "This is my Son, the Beloved . . .; listen to him" (v. 6; compare Matt 3:17). The Matthean scribes, reusing theophany elements in Dan 10, portray the disciples as prostrating themselves in homage (v. 6), but Jesus touches them, saying, "Get up and do not be afraid" (v. 7). They look up and see only Jesus (v. 8); Moses and Elijah have vanished. Their disappearance, of course, is necessary for the narrative; the vision must end so Jesus can continue his mission. It also may have symbolic meaning: disciples who look to Jesus see the fullness of divine revelation, Moses and the prophets included.

The Coming of Elijah (17:9–13)

The discussion on the way down the mountain is taken almost verbatim from Mark 9:9–13. Jesus begins by charging the three disciples to tell no one of their vision "until the Human One has been raised from the dead" (v. 9 AT). The query about why Elijah must come first may seem like a non sequitur. Contemporary readers might ask, what has that to do with resurrection, but that is because we tend to think of *Jesus's* resurrection, whereas the ancient audience during Jesus's lifetime would not have that past experience on which to focus. They would think of the resurrection of the just (e.g., Ezek 36–37), which marks the final judgment, for which Elijah's return is the precursor. Thus, the ancient audience would view Elijah and resurrection as intrinsically connected.

So, Elijah must come first before the resurrection begins, and the Matthean community knew that the resurrection in fact had begun because they knew Jesus was raised. The Markan version of this episode simply states the claim that Elijah has come (Mark 9:9), but the Matthean scribes found that unconvincing. If Elijah had come, where was the evidence? They identify John the Baptist as Elijah returned (11:14), thereby attempting to put at rest their opponents' objections.

Cure of a Boy with Epilepsy (17:14–21)

This healing miracle is an abbreviated version of Mark 9:14–29 focusing on the need for faith. The father asks Jesus to cure his son, who is a "lunatic" (v. 15), that is, someone with epilepsy, which fits were thought to be brought on by the moon. We hear that the disciples tried to cure the boy but were unsuccessful (v. 16). Jesus, exasperated, bemoans the faithless and perverse generation—a group that presumably includes the disciples who failed to cure the boy (v. 17). Jesus calls the child to himself, rebukes the demon, and the boy immediately is cured (v. 18). Later, in private, the disciples ask Jesus why they were not able to cure the child, and he attributes it to their lack of trust (v. 19). Faith even the size of a mustard seed would be sufficient to move mountains; nothing would be impossible (v. 20).

Under the influence of the Markan version of this story, some manuscripts of GMatthew have an addition, v. 21: "But this kind does not come out except by prayer and fasting" (compare to Mark 9:29). However, that verse is not original to GMatthew and undercuts the "moral" of the story about confidence in God.

Second Prediction of the Passion (17:22–23)

The second prediction of Jesus's passion is the most succinct of the set and was likely the first one composed, although the Matthean scribes have put it in the middle of the three predictions. The previous one (Matt 16:21–23) names particular enemies, whereas this one simply states the Human One will be betrayed into human hands. "And they will kill him, and on the third day he will be raised" (17:23a). No debate ensues this time, nor does Peter put himself in the way. Instead, we simply hear that the disciples were deeply grieved.

Payment of the Temple Tax (17:24–27)

We find Jesus and the disciples back in Capernaum, where tax collectors were working. These political functionaries were collecting the didrachma "head tax," obligatory for every adult male Jew, to support the temple in Jerusalem. This story comes from the special Matthean source (M). It highlights Peter as the one initially confronted about payment, as the interlocutor with Jesus on the principle of the tax, and as the one who ends up following through on the payment.

To the officials, Peter affirms that Jesus does pay the tax (vv. 24–25a), but Jesus himself problematizes the issue once Peter returns to the house. The dialogue clearly suggests that the tax is unjust, since the temple belongs to the Jews, who are being treated like aliens in their own land (vv. 25–26). However, "to avoid scandalizing" people, Jesus tells Peter to go fishing: "Go to the sea, drop in a hook, and take the first fish that comes up. Open its mouth and you will find a coin worth twice the temple tax. Give that to them for me and for you" (v. 27). This is an ideal rabbinic solution: In principle, the tax is illegitimate, but in practice, it should be paid. The miracle confirms that God agrees with this solution.

By the time GMatthew is being composed, this tax no longer supported the Jerusalem temple. The Romans destroyed the Jewish temple in 70 CE when they conquered Jerusalem. After the Jewish revolt was finally suppressed, the Romans built a pagan temple on that site and the tax went to pay to support this temple in honor of Jupiter Capitolinus. Such a tax clearly would be offensive to any devout Jew, since it supported pagan worship. Yet the Matthean scribes seem to think it is permissible because it avoids scandal, that is, it prevents any dispute with the Roman officials, who surely could create trouble for the Matthew community.

The Community Discourse

This collection of sayings of Jesus often is called the church order discourse, although it does not include any of the typical items that would appear in a "church order" (e.g., lists of church offices, requirements for and duties of office holders). Since no offices are mentioned, I have called it the community discourse instead, to highlight the focus on intra-community relations.

The Greatest in the Kingdom (18:1–5)

GMatthew presents "the disciples" asking Jesus who is "the greatest" in the *basileia* (compare to Mark 9:33–34). The disciples' concern contradicts Jesus's fundamental message about the reign of God. Jesus does not reprimand them but highlights their misunderstanding by using a toddler as the example.[14] Become like one of these, Jesus says. To a contemporary audience, this sounds sweet and romantic; to an ancient audience, it would be shocking

14. The Greek word here, *paidion*, is a diminutive form, usually translated "little child." The root word, *pais*, can refer to a child or a slave, so "little slave" would be an alternative translation.

and offensive. Children had no rights, and child mortality rates were high enough that those below five years old tended to be discounted, at least by those who valued persons according to the work they could contribute. A small child was of less economic value than a slave, since slaves contributed work, but toddlers required the work of others. Jesus might as well have said "become like the destitute" (see also 19:21), for they are the "greatest" in God's realm. Jesus turns the whole category of "greatness" on its head (see also Luke 1:52–53). As will be made clear later, those who would be "great" must be willing to become the slave of all (Matt 20:26).

Temptation (18:6–9)

The concept of smallness provides the segue to this saying about leading "small people" into temptation. Jesus does not mean to imply that it is fine to tempt strong people, yet the stouthearted are not likely to succumb. The "small" ones here are not small of stature but rather new converts, simple minded, or otherwise at risk of falling away. Anyone who puts a stumbling block (*skandalon*) in their way should be drowned alive (18:6). Jesus bemoans "the world" that puts such roadblocks in the way of the innocent. Such tests "must come," that is, one can learn to overcome temptations only by being tested, but woe to those who put such temptations in others' way (v. 7). The final two verses repeat the injunction of Matt 5:29–30 to cut off your hand or foot or tear out your eye if it "scandalizes" you, causing you to stumble (18:8–9).

The Lost Sheep (18:10–14)

Returning to the "small people," this section reinforces the idea that God especially protects the weak and meek. No one should despise them. After all, the little ones have guardian angels who "constantly behold" God's face and thereby intercede for their protection (18:10–11). The subsequent Q parable (18:12–14; see also Luke 15:3–7) about the lost sheep displays God's persistence in caring for the little ones, to ensure that none be lost in the end.[15]

15. This term for "lost" (*apoletai*) has apocalyptic overtones and refers to being utterly destroyed, in this case, one who is condemned at the final judgment.

A Community Member Who Missteps (18:15–20)

The discourse then turns to the question of how to handle a community member who engages in inappropriate behavior.[16] The passage builds one intervention upon another as the problem is seen to escalate, starting with one community member confronting the offender (v. 15), increasing to two or three persons making the intervention (v. 16; compare Deut 19:15). If that does not work, the issue should be brought before the entire congregation (Matt 18:17a). If the individual refuses to correct the behavior even when confronted by the congregation, then the person is to be shunned, treated "as a Gentile and a tax collector" (v. 17b).

This last line, so contrary to Jesus's own behavior in calling the "tax collector" whose name appears on this gospel, suggests that this section was developed by the Matthean community while they were trying to deal with the stresses of community life after the resurrection. Sections like this are framed as teachings from Jesus himself because they are the fruits of the inspired community's reflection on the life and teaching of Jesus. It is not only a matter of "this is what Jesus would say *if* he were here with us." The believing and worshiping community experienced the risen Jesus present in their midst (v. 20).[17] So, when they were reflecting on how to adapt the example and teaching of Jesus to their present situation, they saw the spirit of Jesus as leading their reflections and guiding their decisions.

The section on "binding and loosing" (18:18–19) repeats nearly verbatim the earlier episode (16:19) where Simon Peter is given "the keys to the *basileia*" (AT) and the disciples are given the authority to bind and loose. Here it is made clear that the authority is given to the believing community as a whole, not an individual or set of individuals within that community.

16. The Greek word *hamartia* typically is translated "sin," but it is an archery term that refers to missing the target. It can refer to a positive moral error of some sort (a "sin") or to some other more or less serious faux pas (an error or even a social misstep). I have construed the term as indicating a broader category of unacceptable behaviors.

Some of the less important New Testament codices include "against you [sg.]" after *hamartia*, but the best witnesses do not include that limiting language. The entire passage throughout refers to the individual "you," not the group.

17. This understanding of divine presence is not unique to GMatthew. Compare the Matthean promise "where two or three are gathered" (Matt 18:20) with a saying from a second-century rabbi in Pirqê 'Abôt 3.3: "When two sit and there are between them the words of the Torah, the divine presence [*Shekinah*] rests upon them."

The Unforgiving Servant (18:21–35)

The final section in this discourse focuses on the dynamics of forgiveness. Starting with a question from Peter (now going by the nickname Jesus gave him in 16:18), the initial premise seems to be not so much "How many times must I forgive?" but rather "How few times?" or "Where can I draw the line?" If we give Peter's words a generous interpretation, his suggestion of "seven times" (18:21) may be intended to convey perfection, whereas Jesus's response takes it to the superlative level (v. 22).[18]

The following parable drives home both the astounding profligacy of divine forgiveness and the requirement that those who have been forgiven also will "pay it forward" to those who need to be forgiven. The history of interpretation tends to spiritualize this teaching, but note that the parable involves *debt* forgiveness and focuses on enormous economic disparities.

The monarch calls in the notes of those to whom he has lent money. One debtor owed ten thousand talents (v. 24); an astronomical sum larger than the GNP of many countries today.[19] Not surprisingly, the debtor has no way to pay back the loan, so the lender orders that the debtor, his wife, and his children be sold into slavery as partial payment of the debt (v. 25). Combined, they would not have been worth one talent, so this is a pitiful return on investment, but it was the routine legal way of dealing with those who default on loans. The debtor begs for time, asserting that he will pay the debt in full—a flagrant lie, perhaps to himself as well as the lender. Astoundingly, the monarch has pity and forgives the loan.

The one whose debt was forgiven calls in the note of someone to whom he had lent the significantly smaller sum of one hundred denarii (v. 28).[20] This debtor also begs for time, telling at least a possible truth when he promises to pay back the loan (v. 29). Instead of showing pity, the forgiven debtor has the second one thrown into debtors' prison until the entire loan is repaid (v. 30).

This would have been the end of the line for many people in Jesus's day, but the parable continues by highlighting the disturbed reactions of other servants. They take the tale to the monarch, who is predictably outraged (v. 31). The ruler summons the first debtor and berates the person for

18. Some commentators have pointed to a possible reversal here of the vengeance of Lamech (Gen 4:24). The gospel of Jesus replaces vengeance with mercy.

19. Assuming these were silver talents, the financial equivalency is approximately sixteen thousand years' wages, over $700,000,000 at a minimum wage of $15/hour.

20. This is equivalent to one hundred days' wages in the time of Jesus; it equals about $12,000 at a minimum wage of $15/hour.

such pitiless behavior (v. 32–33). In an unusual move, showing the fury of the overlord's response to the ill treatment of the second debtor, the unforgiving debtor is arrested and handed over "to be tortured until he would pay his entire debt" (v. 34)—an endless sentence since the astronomical size of the debt would make it impossible to pay off.

The parable ends with a moralizing warning: God will do the same (at the final judgment), withdrawing forgiveness from those who refuse to show mercy. Again, the spiritual aspect of mercy is important, but so is the economic aspect, which is the central focus of this parable of Jesus. Those who refuse to forgive debts or who set themselves up in judgment of the poor, presuming to show charity toward only those they decide are "deserving" of it, will face judgment and retribution from God.

End of GMatthew Book 4 (19:1)

This fourth book of Jesus concludes with the same formula as noted earlier: "When Jesus had finished saying these things . . ." (19:1a). A change of venue is noted: the next part of Jesus's ministry will take place not in Galilee but in Judea (v. 1b).

Conclusions

This fourth book of Jesus in GMatthew heightens the conflict between Jesus and some of his Jewish opponents and also heightens the demands of discipleship. The execution of John the Baptist and the first two predictions of the passion appear in this section, as do conflict vignettes with groups of scribes, Pharisees, and Sadducees, who are reprimanded for demanding a sign of Jesus's authenticity. Transplanted post-resurrection appearances and nature miracles provide the disciples with the evidence these outsiders demanded. Feeding and healing miracles on both sides of the Sea of Galilee, and healings as far afield as the region of Tyre and Sidon, show that Jesus is opening his ministry to gentiles as well as Jews, although he remains focused on "the lost sheep of the house of Israel" (15:24). The narrative includes elements where Jesus is shown handing off some of his authority to the disciples, including the power to "bind and loose" (16:19; 18:18) and to do miracles, although the disciples are shown as unsuccessful in the latter regard (17:16). The section concludes with a series of teachings on forgiveness of interpersonal offenses; correction of public misbehavior; and remission of debts. True to the historical teaching of Jesus, GMatthew pays particular attention to this last point about debt forgiveness, applying a warning of condemnation at the final judgment for those who refuse to show mercy in explicit economic behaviors.

Review and Discussion Questions

A. Review Questions

1. What are some of the symbolic features of the two stories of Jesus feeding the multitudes (chs. 14–15)?
2. What are the key features of the scene of Simon Peter's confession of faith in Jesus as Messiah (Matt 16:13–20)?
3. Like Jesus's preaching elsewhere (including the Lord's Prayer), the parable of the unforgiving servant (Matt 18:21–35) focuses on economics, specifically, forgiveness of debts. What is the central message of this parable, according to GMatthew?

B. Discussion Questions

1. What are some of the more striking features of the story of the cure of the Canaanite woman's daughter (Matt 15:21–28)? What do you see as the key takeaways from that scene?
2. GMatthew frequently presents Jesus in disputes with "the Pharisees" and other groups within Judaism of his day (e.g., the Sadducees, the Herodians). What purpose would those disputes have served for the original audience? What might a contemporary audience need to remember when reading those disputes today?
3. The Matthean scribes seem to reinterpret Jesus's prediction of the parousia (quoted in Matt 16:28) so they can avoid portraying Jesus as making a false prediction. What do you think of this move? Do you think the evangelists should have left Jesus's prediction stand as it was (as we see in GMark), without correcting it? Does it bother you to think of Jesus being mistaken?
4. The parable of the unforgiving servant condemns those who refuse to forgive debts and set themselves up in judgment of the poor; those who show charity only toward persons they view as "deserving" will face divine wrath. Where do you see these kinds of judgmental behaviors toward the poor today? What social and economic policies would need to be changed to redress this situation?

Chapter 7

MINISTRY IN JUDEA AND JERUSALEM

(Matt 19–23)

As the gospel aims toward its climax, the scene shifts from Galilee to Judea. Jesus goes there via Perea, on the east side of the Sea of Galilee (Matt 19:1b), rather than heading more or less directly south through Samaria—a rather pointed way of demonstrating that those in the region of Samaria do not count as "real" Jews in the mindset of the Matthean scribes who composed this narrative. Taking his message to the heart of Jewish identity raises the risk for Jesus; neither the religious nor political leaders in Jerusalem would be happy to hear of a divine *basileia* that will replace their existing power structures. While Jesus remains popular with the crowds, among whom he continues his healing activity (v. 2), this section of the gospel includes an increased number of confrontations between Jesus and other Jewish interest groups.

Contested Questions

Contesting a Husband's Right to Divorce (19:3–12)

English translations of GMatthew typically entitle this section as if the topic were marriage and divorce generically conceived, but that ignores the specific framing of the question posed to Jesus. The narrator says "some Pharisees" asked Jesus, "Is it lawful for a man to divorce his wife for any cause?" (v. 3) So, the question does not concern divorce as it is construed nowadays, with either party having the right to initiate divorce proceedings. In fact, that situation is quite a recent development. Rather, the question posed to Jesus concerns the husband's unilateral divorce of his wife "for any cause" he deems valid. The question invokes a first-century debate among various interpretive traditions, most notably connected with the rabbis Shammai and Hillel. The question aligns with the Hillel school of interpretation, whereas the tradition from Shammai insisted that the husband could divorce his wife only in the case of adultery. It is not clear why the Matthean scribes pose this question as a "test" of Jesus, which language usually implies a rhetorical trap. If the challenge was intended to discover whether Jesus took a "liberal" or "conservative" view of the husband's right to divorce, he shows himself instead to be a radical.

Jesus's basic response to this question is no. He not only rejects the sweeping claim of a husband's right unilaterally to end a marriage "for any cause"; he rejects the premise that a husband has a right to end his marriage at all. Period. Under any circumstances. This puts Jesus beyond not only the "liberal" view of Hillel but also the "conservative" ruling of Shammai. Jesus rejects the premise that a husband has unilateral authority in the marital relationship. When commentators categorize the traditions of Hillel and Shammai as "liberal" and "conservative," respectively, they are viewing the relationship from the husband's side. While this bias may be understandable, since it is how the question is posed to Jesus, it misleads the reader; Jesus rejects precisely that perspective.

Jesus's response considers the wife's side of the question. She is legally powerless and is not even viewed as a person given the way the question was framed. But Jesus does not accept this framework, which dehumanizes "the wife." He uses a midrashic interpretation, innovatively combining two elements of the Genesis creation stories (specifically, Gen 1:27 and 2:24) to create new grounds for a woman's rights in marriage. No, her husband cannot unilaterally end her marriage, regardless of how frivolous or serious a reason he may think he has (Matt 19:4–6). Given that GMatthew depicts Jesus's own mother as nearly being divorced by her betrothed husband (1:19), perhaps this family history has had some affect upon Jesus's thinking. Still, he shows a concern for the "least" in all sorts of situations, so his protectiveness is not unique.

The narrative continues with a second challenge from the questioners (v. 7): How can you say such a thing when Moses commanded that a man give the woman a bill of divorce and dismiss her? Jesus attributes this Mosaic ruling to "hardness of heart" (v. 8), that is, the man's refusal to conform himself to the mercy of God. In another innovative move, Jesus further asserts that any man who "divorces his wife . . . and marries another commits adultery" (v. 9); the previous biblical tradition defined "adultery" as a violation of a *husband's* rights. A married woman committed adultery by having sex outside of marriage, but a husband did not; a man committed adultery only by having sex with another man's wife. This teaching eliminates the double standard concerning adultery.

Thus far, the story here agrees with the Markan version (Mark 10:1–12), but the Matthean community adds another section to this vignette. The male disciples object to Jesus's teaching (v. 10): Then it's better not to marry at all! If a husband does not have univocal control over "his" wife, then what's the point? This objection now positions the male disciples in the same camp as Jesus's initial challengers—a rather remarkable but clever move on the narrator's part that brings the audience into the debate. The Matthean scribes depict Jesus agreeing that marriage is not for everyone (v. 11) and also affirming that some are called to celibacy "for the sake of the *basileia*" (v. 12 AT).

A few words may be in order about the contemporary application of this teaching. The prohibition about a man unilaterally divorcing his wife ought not to be taken as a blanket prohibition of divorce per se. There are times when a couple reaches a mutual agreement to end a marriage that has become damaging to both parties. While one might argue that this arises from "hardness of heart," that kind of generalization disrespects the facts of individual cases. Jesus was trying to avoid the exploitation of the weaker party in the ancient marital relationship; that's what this teaching forbids. Such exploitation can happen as a result of divorce, but it also can happen within marriage. Jesus's teaching here forbids exploitation in either situation.

Blessing the Children (19:13–52)

The disciples try to prevent some little children pestering Jesus, but he reprimands the disciples, commanding them to allow the children access. Jesus blesses the children and repeats his remarks of the previous vignette (18:2–4) in which he used a toddler as representative of the *basileia*.

The Rich Youth (19:16–30)

A rich youth comes to Jesus and asks what "good thing" he must do to enter the *basileia* (v. 16). This is not quite such a generic question as first appears. "Good thing" is an expression meaning *mitzvah*, righteous deed commanded or implied by Torah. Jesus reframes the question as one that reflects divine goodness and then goes on to tie the youth's query directly to the commandments, in particular those in the Decalogue (19:17–19). A little flippantly, perhaps showing his immature age, the young man asserts he has done all those—as if they form a checklist that, once done, can be passed over—and asks what more he should do (v. 20). Jesus replies that he should sell all his possessions, give the proceeds to the poor, and become a disciple (v. 21). But the youth went away grieving, refusing the invitation, for he had many possessions (v. 22).

Jesus draws a wider interpretation from this individual case, using the hyperbole of a camel passing through a needle's eye to highlight how difficult it is for a rich person to enter the *basileia* (19:23–24). Again, the disciples are said to object to such a countercultural point of view (v. 25): Who then can be saved? They (wrongly) assume that wealth proves divine favor and therefore guarantees a place in the *basileia*.[1] The fallback line, that all things are possible for God (v. 26), does not deny the earlier demand to reject wealth; it simply calls all disciples to rely upon divine mercy rather than trying to enter into some sort of accounting system with God.

Ironically, Peter immediately is depicted as trying to do something very much like that accounting system: "We have given up everything to follow you; what then will we get?" (v. 27 AT). One imagines Jesus rolling his eyes and sighing at this self-serving question. Nevertheless, Jesus gives a reassuring response: You twelve will judge the tribes of Israel at the final judgment, and everyone who has given up house, family, or lands for the sake of the gospel will receive a hundredfold reward (19:28–29).

The final remark in this section (v. 30), taken from Mark 10:31, highlights the reversal of expectations. The *basileia* is not what people have thought. It does not replicate the economic disparities and class consciousness of the present sociopolitical system. Rather, it is a reality in which rank is eliminated, the first put last and the last first, and no one has any claims

1. This mistaken teaching later becomes part of the doctrine of John Calvin and has morphed perversely into the so-called "prosperity gospel," which violates the gospel of Jesus in every particular.

because all is the gift of God. This leads directly into the parable of the workers, which illustrates the adage about first and last.

Workers in the Vineyard (20:1–16)

The Parable of the Workers is unique to GMatthew so attributed to the M source. The story goes through various phases of the vineyard owner hiring workers for the harvest, some quite early in the morning, some midmorning, some at noon, some midafternoon, and some quite late in the day (20:1–7). The narrator states that the first group agreed to be paid a denarius for the day (the usual daily wage [v. 2]), but the later workers are simply told they will receive "whatever is right" (v. 4). When the day draws to a close, those hired last are paid first, and they receive a full day's wage (vv. 8–9). This generosity leads the first hires to expect they will be paid more than the agreed amount (v. 10); when that expectation is disappointed, they grumble against the landowner (vv. 11–12). The owner falls back on their initial contract negotiation, pointing out they were paid at the agreed rate (v. 13). What grounds have they to complain? "Am I not allowed to do what I choose with what belongs to me? Or are you envious because I am generous?" (v. 15). The adage about the reversal of first and last is repeated as a sort of "moral" to the parable (v. 16), thereby providing bookends both before and after it.

The parable is designed to lead the audience to identify with the first hires and to expect pay proportional to the time spent at harvesting, even though they had agreed to the one-denarius daily wage. If the first hires were paid first and then went away, the appearance of a pay disparity would not have arisen. But the last hires were paid first, ensuring that all the other hires would know that they received a denarius, a full day's wage. With the first hires, we would expect a bonus over that one denarius rate. Proportionality also could have been maintained if the last hires got only 10 percent of the full day's wage. But that is not the way the story plays out. Every worker gets a full day's pay, regardless of how long they spent harvesting the grapes. This one day's pay was sufficient for the person to eat enough to survive until the next day. When accusing the first hires of "envy," the landowner implies that they would not want the last hires to receive even a subsistence wage—an unfair implication, but parables are not designed to be fair. They are designed to get the audience engaged, often by provoking a strong emotional reaction.

The landowner's insistence on the freedom "to do what I choose with what belongs to me" has been critiqued by postcolonial interpreters as elitist. Landowners of Jesus's time tended to be Roman client rulers or other elite families who had gained control of the land by exploiting the poor, including day laborers who worked at harvesttime. However, the accusation of elitism seems less appropriate for this parable. Key to this story is the landowner's decision to giving every worker a subsistence wage rather than paying the later workers less.

For a Jewish audience, the vineyard imagery would immediately raise connections with earlier Bible texts that represent Israel as God's vineyard (e.g., Isa 5:1–7; Ps 80:8–10), although the primary focus of the parable is the action of the harvest rather than its location. As is the case with other Matthean parables, this one seems particularly suited to an allegorical interpretation, with God as the vineyard owner, Israel as the vineyard, and the various workers at different stages of the harvest as the prophets and now, at the final hour of the day, the disciples of Jesus. Everyone who works in this divine harvest reaps the same reward of inclusion in the coming *basileia*.

The Third Prediction of the Passion (20:17–19)

The vineyard parable is followed immediately by this third and final prediction of Jesus's passion and death. The narrator follows GMark in setting this prediction on the road "up to Jerusalem" (Matt 20:17; Mark 10:32). Jesus takes the Twelve aside to give them the most detailed of the three predictions (16:21–23; 17:22–23). It warns of the Human One being handed over to the chief priests and scribes and condemned (20:18); then being handed over to gentiles to be mocked, scourged, and crucified (v. 19; see also Matt 27:2, 26–31, 35). GMatthew omits the Markan reference to being spat upon but otherwise follows the Markan version nearly verbatim. The other key differences are that GMatthew specifies that Jesus will be put to death *by crucifixion* and that *he will be raised up* (rather than rise) on the third day.

Self-Aggrandizement of James and John (20:20–28)

The following scene with James and John seems particularly appalling given the placement right after Jesus has warned the Twelve of his impending betrayal and execution. The narrative reflects the intermixing of the historical trajectory of Jesus's life with the hindsight available to the

Matthean community after all those events had taken place. On the road to Jerusalem, the first disciples would not have had specific warnings from Jesus about what would transpire in the Holy City. On the contrary, they had every reason to think that Jesus would be acclaimed as the Messiah-King of Israel, including laying claim to the throne of his ancestor David (Matt 21:1–11, esp. v. 9). In that context, the brothers' request to be appointed as Jesus's viceroys still looks self-serving but not callous.

GMatthew tries to downplay the embarrassment of this scene by making their mother the one who approaches Jesus for this favor rather than the two men themselves (compare Mark 10:35–45). Still, in the honor-shame society of the first-century Greco-Roman world, the men are shamed by having a woman make the appeal rather than themselves taking the action.[2] Jesus's response (vv. 22–28) is addressed to the men, as is made clear by the plural forms of the verbs. This may simply result from the Matthean scribes following the Markan version of the story, or it may be a more pointed strategy to show that the Matthean Jesus is aware who put the mother up to asking for this outrageous favor.

The response attributed to Jesus is as blunt as such a request deserves: You don't have any idea what you two are asking. Can you accept the end that I am getting ready to meet? (v. 22). The two men assert that they can, but the audience soon will see that in fact they flee when the time comes. Jesus rebukes the men, reminding them that God is the one who establishes ruling authority in the coming *basileia*; it is not for Jesus to delegate (v. 23).

The other ten members of the Twelve hear about what James and John have done and, reasonably enough, are indignant at their hubris. Jesus summons all of the Twelve to confront them about their wrongheaded view of what discipleship means. They are mimicking how power is projected by the rulers and elite among "the gentiles" (i.e., the Romans and their client kings and supporters); but God does not work that way. "You know that the rulers of the Gentiles lord it over them, and their great ones are tyrants over them. It will not be so among you, but whoever wishes to be great among you must be your servant" (vv. 25b–26). Because they have shown such resistance to this message in the past, Jesus repeats and heightens that second part of his admonition: "Whoever wishes to be first among you shall be your slave" (v. 27). Returning to himself as the example, he affirms that

2. Some commentators think this modification may be under the influence of 1 Kgs 1:11–21, where Bathsheba is portrayed as approaching David to request that he make Solomon heir to his kingdom.

"the Human One" (Jesus himself) came not to be served but to serve and give his life for "the many," that is, for everyone, including those who are unimportant and powerless in the eyes of the elite (v. 28).

Speech-Acts of Jesus

The next section of the gospel includes a series of miracles (both positive and, unusually, a negative one) as well as some actions that convey prophetic messages. Such actions are called "speech-acts" because of the way the message is embedded in the action itself. These kinds of actions show Jesus as a prophet in the lineage of the great prophets of Israel, especially Elijah, Elisha, Jeremiah, and Ezekiel. The Matthean scribes certainly see Jesus as "a greater" than all these ancient prophetic leaders, but it is helpful to their ancient audience to have some points of comparison for understanding the full reality represented by Jesus.

Healing of Two Blind Persons (20:29–34)

The narrative placement of this healing of the sight-impaired persons is particularly pointed. In the previous scene, the Twelve were presented as clueless about Jesus's true mission and how it would culminate, in spite of the warnings and predictions the Matthean Jesus gave them. The gift of sight to the blind metaphorically displays what it takes to truly understand the person and mission of Jesus. The sight-impaired persons hear Jesus in their vicinity. Afraid he will simply bypass them, they call out to him for mercy (v. 30). Like the two blind persons, one who would follow Jesus must recognize him as the one who can "let our eyes be opened" (v. 33). Once sight is restored, following Jesus is the only appropriate response (v. 34), even when following him means going "up to Jerusalem" to face death with him.

Entering Jerusalem (21:1–11)

Jesus and the disciples come to the outskirts of Jerusalem, to a place called Bethphage, which the Matthean scribes locate on the Mount of Olives (21:1; Zech 14:4).[3] Following the Markan story, the narrator says Jesus

3. No precise site has been identified, although there is a church on the Mount of Olives that marks a traditional spot. It is possible that the name is at least as symbolic as pragmatic, since the Hebrew name means "house of unripe figs." Since Mark 11:1

sent two of his companions to the village to retrieve a donkey they would find tied there. In accord with the Matthean scribes' habit of doubling characters, the emissaries will find not one animal but two, a mother and foal (v. 2). If anyone challenges them about taking the animals, they should reply that "the Lord" (*kyrios*) needs them (v. 3). The Matthean scribes tie this event to Zechariah's description of the coming of the messianic King (Matt 21:4–5; citing Zech 9:9).

The two disciples bring the two animals, cover them with cloaks (the plural of *himation* is used), and the narrative makes it sound like Jesus somehow rode both animals (Matt 21:6–7). This editorial glitch seems to arise from a misunderstanding of the Hebrew poetic doublet in Zech 9:9; after all, Jesus is not a circus rider standing on their backs, nor could someone really straddle two animals side by side without causing oneself rather painful injury. The Matthean scribes must have meant to convey that Jesus sat astride the mother donkey while the foal followed closely alongside. The inclusion of the foal heightens the peaceful character of this coming king; not only is Jesus's mount a donkey rather than a warhorse, it is a nursing mother with her child.

The narrator mentions "the greatest crowd" gathering and making a symbolic carpet on the road by laying down their cloaks and tree branches for Jesus to ride upon (v. 8). They form a procession before and after Jesus, quoting Ps 118:25–26 and crying, "Hosanna to the Son of David; blessed the one coming in the name of the Lord" (v. 9 AT). While invoking the coming of divine salvation, the crowd's acclamation also attributes messianic kingly identity to Jesus.

This rather flamboyant entry is said to rock the city of Jerusalem; inhabitants wonder who is this person who has caused such a tumult.[4] The audience of GMatthew already knows Jesus, but the gospel narrative presents this as his first appearance in the city. Jesus's prior ministry has taken place in Galilee and other regions beyond Judea, so we get the sense that this is his first exposure to the people of Jerusalem. They are not necessarily opposed to Jesus, but the scene implies they are nervous and perhaps more than a bit frightened of him.

---

mentions it before Bethany, the evangelists seem to think it is a bit east of Bethany on the approach to the Holy City.

4. The same term is used here as in Matt 27:51, when referring to the earthquake at the time of the crucifixion, and also in Matt 28:4 in reference to the terror of the guards at Jesus's tomb when the angel appeared to them.

Some of the crowd respond to the query about Jesus's identity in a rather understated way: "This is the prophet Jesus from Nazareth in Galilee" (v. 11). The earlier acclamation, however, identified Jesus as the messianic King; classifying him as a prophet makes him less of a threat to the Jerusalem power structure. The mention of Galilee is more ominous, not merely a place identification. The previous first-century messiah figures came from Galilee, most notably Judas the Galilean (fl. ca. 6 CE). Anyone who remembered the tax revolt under Judas would not have been reassured by Jesus's connection with Galilee.

Cleansing the Temple (21:12–17)

Upon entering the Holy City, the Matthean Jesus goes straight to the temple (v. 12). This modifies the Markan timeline, in which Jesus enters the city, scopes out the temple area, and withdraws to Bethany for the night (Mark 11:11). The Matthean itinerary is politically wiser. Why waste the political capital of the crowd if you want to assert control of the temple? Having Jesus claim ownership of that sacred space while he still has support of the mob is a safer move.

Jesus is said to have expelled "all who were selling and buying" in the outer court of the temple (the Court of the Gentiles), including overturning the tables of the money changers (Matt 21:12). The scribal tradition (taken from Mark 11:17) uses a quotation from Isa 56:7 to justify this reclamation of "my . . . house of prayer" from those who have made it "a den of brigands" (Matt 21:13 AT). The reference to brigands, and this entire episode depicting Jesus as overturning tables and driving out those who were, after all, providing a necessary service to pilgrims, may be influenced by events of the First Jewish Revolt (66–73 CE) rather than details of the life of Jesus himself. The revolutionaries did indeed take over the temple as their base of operations, thereby making it "a den of brigands"—at least from the vantage point of those who opposed the rebellion. In that case, overturning the tables and eliminating the currency exchange (necessary to avoid using idolatrous coinage for the purchase of sacrificial animals) would symbolize the Roman destruction of the temple when the revolt was suppressed. In other words, this part of the story may represent another case where the Matthean scribes are using the story of Jesus not to relate what he himself did but rather to show what he *would* have done a generation later if given the opportunity to confront the false messiahs leading the revolt.

The Markan scene concludes rather abruptly after this story of Jesus overturning the tables, moving quickly to indicate a plot to kill Jesus on the part of "the chief priests and scribes" (Mark 11:18) and having Jesus and his companions leave the city to spend the night elsewhere. The Matthean scribes are clearly not satisfied with such a stenographic and theologically confusing presentation, so they expand the scene in the temple.

Their additional segment (Matt 21:14–17) shows Jesus enacting the *basileia* message he has been preaching, which fits very well with the life and ministry of the historical Jesus. In fact, the audience would notice nothing amiss if Matt 21:12–13 were simply omitted from the gospel narrative altogether and the temple scene began with v. 14. Jesus sets up operations in the temple precincts (presumably the outer court, where teaching and other non-sacrificial activities could take place) and continues his healing ministry. In particular, "the blind and lame" are named as recipients of this healing power, which restores to wholeness persons whose physical ailments might have interfered with their worship in the temple.[5]

Jesus again is acclaimed as "Son of David" by onlookers (the term *paidas*, referring to the speakers, may be translated either as children or slaves), reaffirming the assertion of the processional crowd that Jesus was the long-awaited Messiah-King. This acclamation is said to unsettle "the chief priests and the scribes" (v. 15), and they challenge Jesus about it.[6] The Matthean scribes construct a defense, using the Septuagint version of Ps 8:3 to justify such praise coming from the mouths of the simple. It is not clear whether the audience is expected to think the quotation mollified those who objected to this title for Jesus. The narrator simply ends the dispute at that point, noting that Jesus left the Holy City and returned to Bethany for the night (v. 17).

Cursing the Fig Tree (21:18–22)

Returning to Jerusalem the next morning, Jesus is depicted as doing the only miracle in his repertory that harms something: He curses a fig tree

5. Leviticus 21:16–21 excludes disabled priests from engaging in temple duties, but it is not clear whether this restriction was applied more broadly in the time of Jesus.

6. Again, there seems to be an editorial glitch here. The chief priests and scribes are described as upset by both Jesus's miraculous healings and his acclamation as Son of David (v. 15), yet the challenge focuses exclusively on the title (v. 16). The concern about the title alone makes much better sense, since it poses a direct challenge to Roman political power.

to death. The Matthean version is shocking, although Jesus is depicted in a somewhat better light than in the earlier Markan story (Mark 11:12–14, 20–25), which blithely mentions that it was not the right season for figs. Rather than making Jesus look arbitrary, the Matthean scribes omit that detail. In the Matthean story, Jesus is hungry and looks to the fig tree for a snack but finds none; Jesus curses the tree, which instantly shrivels and dies before their very eyes (Matt 21:18–19). The narrator speaks of the disciples' astonishment—not at the fact that Jesus killed the tree but at the speed with which the curse took effect (v. 21). (This is the other key modification from the Markan version, in which the tree dies several hours later.) In riposte, Jesus repeats what was said earlier about faith that can move mountains (Matt 17:20).

Like the scene with the Canaanite woman (Matt 15:21–28), Jesus does not appear at his best here. Cursing a fruitless tree because he didn't have breakfast? While there may be days when we have a similar impulse, it seems petty for Jesus to act this way. The scene is likely to be historical—after all, what believer would concoct a story showing Jesus so ill tempered—but the Matthean scribes likely included it to convey a figurative meaning. The fruitless tree and the city of Jerusalem are connected in the narrative. The final harvest is imminent, the *basileia* soon to be revealed. As a prophetic speech-act, the curse of the fig tree illustrates what may happen to Jerusalem if the inhabitants do not show the proper "fruits" required of the chosen people.

Challenges and Parables

GMatthew turns to a series of five controversies between Jesus and the religious authorities in Jerusalem. Each controversy highlights what is at stake in the choice to follow Jesus or to thwart his mission.

The Authority of Jesus (21:23–27)

This scene finds Jesus in the temple again, now engaged in teaching. The chief priests come to Jesus, this time in company with "the elders," and challenge his authority for doing "these things" (v. 23). The vignette comprises a doublet with what appeared a few verses earlier (21:15–16), when Jesus first took control of the temple precincts, and follows the Markan version almost verbatim (Mark 11:27–33).

Rather than providing an answer to the question about his authority, Jesus puts the challengers to the test by posing a counterquestion about the origins of John the Baptist's authority (Matt 21:24–25a). The omniscient narrator lets the audience overhear the opponents' huddled conversation. Rather than seriously discerning what role God played in the mission of John, the challengers are presented as viewing the entire exchange as a game of one-upmanship: "If we say, [John's baptism was] 'From heaven,' he will say to us, 'Why, then, did you not believe him?' But if we say, 'Of human origin,' we are afraid of the crowd, for all regard John as a prophet"(21:25b–26). In the end, they decline to state an opinion. Since they sidestep providing an authoritative ruling on John, Jesus refuses to honor their question about the source of his own authority (v. 27). The audience, of course, knows the true answers: Both John's and Jesus's missions were authorized by God, although the religious authorities in Jerusalem recognized neither one.

Two Children (21:28–32)

This parable is one of three in a sequence that focuses on the judgment of Israel. This first story is unique to GMatthew, deriving from M.

A parent with two children commands them both to work in the family vineyard. The first child refuses to obey but later repents and goes to work (vv. 28–29). The second child agrees to the command but does not follow through on that commitment (v. 30). In the honor-shame culture of the first-century Roman world, the first child shamed the parent by refusing, while the second one honored the parent by agreeing to obey the command. Jesus's question, however, focuses not on honor-shame dynamics but on who "did the will" of the parent (v. 31a). The audience has to admit that, in spite of the initial refusal, the first child enacted the parent's will.

The Matthean scribes use the story as a springboard to a saying of Jesus about who is welcome in the *basileia*. The riffraff of Jewish society ("tax collectors and prostitutes") are entering the *basileia* before the religious leaders ("you") because they believed John and followed "the way of righteousness" that John taught, but the leaders did not accept John even after proof of his divine authorization (vv. 31b–32).

Vineyard Tenants (21:33–46)

This second parable in the sequence is drawn from Mark 12:1–12, although the Matthean version is more highly allegorized.[7]

The Matthean scribes use this parable to present an allegory about the final "harvest." As in the earlier parable about the vineyard harvesters (20:1–16), this story is used to convey a message about God (the landowner) and Israel (the vineyard). Instead of paid harvesters, this parable depicts the land as leased to tenant farmers who were to pay the landowner a portion of their harvest as rent. At harvesttime, the landowner sent slaves to collect the payments owed, to no avail. The slaves were beaten, abused, even killed (v. 34–35). Sending a larger number of slaves did not help; they suffered the same fate (v. 36). Finally, the landowner sent the heir to the estate, thinking the tenants would show respect; instead, they resolved to kill the son so the land would default to their possession (vv. 37–39). Jesus asks the audience what the landowner will do when hearing about the murder of the son, and they admit that the vicious tenants will be executed and the lands leased to others who will honor their commitment (21:40–41).

The story as it stands would be totally believable for either Jesus's audience or the Matthean community. They would be amply familiar with tenant farmers, absentee landowners, hostile tenants—the whole cast of characters here. So also would they know of reprisals against tenants who violated contracts and murdered heirs. The parable is designed to make the audience sympathize with the landowner against the faithless tenants.

The allegorical interpretation builds on this sympathy to help the audience see the situation from God's point of view. The slaves sent by the landowner are the prophets and other faithful leaders of Israel; the tenants are individual members of the tribes of Israel, perhaps especially the leaders who oppose Jesus; the owner's son, of course, is Jesus himself. The Matthean scribes do not outline this allegorical interpretation, but they certainly expect their audience to draw these basic parallels.

Jesus confronts the leaders of the people, "I say to you, the *basileia* of God will be taken away from you and given to a people who will produce its fruit" (v. 43 AT). The narrator mentions that "the chief priests and the Pharisees" saw themselves as the targets of this parable (v. 45) and responded by trying to arrest Jesus; they were not successful because the crowds viewed Jesus as a prophet (v. 46).

7. A less allegorized version also appears in Gos. Thom. 65.

The Wedding Feast (22:1–14)

The parable of the wedding feast, unique to GMatthew, is also attributed to the M source. Like other parables in M, it seems intended more as an allegory than a parable, strictly speaking. The various characters beg to be construed as representing other figures outside the storyline. The king (*basileius*), the son, the servants, the invitees, all sound familiar to those who know the history of Israel. A Jewish audience would certainly identify the king as God, the son as the Israelite monarch, the servants as the prophets, and the invitees as the whole people of Israel. The fact that the initial invitees refused the invitation would reinforce those initial identifications. The mistreatment and even murder of the second wave of servants (v. 6) would remind the Matthean audience of the tradition that "all" the prophets had been murdered by their ancestors, while the monarch's invasion and destruction of "their city" (v. 7) would bring back tales of the Babylonian conquest for Jesus's original audience and vivid memories of the Roman destruction of Jerusalem for the later Matthean community. All of these details from the first half of the parable would resonate with the early audiences.

The second part of the parable (vv. 8–14) poses more of a challenge. The original invitees, who refused to attend the wedding feast, are now excluded; the servants are told to give their places to others, "whomever you find" (v. 9) at the crossroads. The servants do as commanded, bringing to the feast both the good and the evil (v. 10).[8] The king comes to the feast and finds that one of the guests is inappropriately dressed (v. 11); the guest is challenged for having entered without wedding garments but, dumbfounded, makes no reply (v. 12). The king commands the servants to bind and cast that guest "into the darkness outside, where there will be wailing and grinding of teeth" (v. 13). The parable ends with the punch line "Many are invited, but few are chosen" (v. 14).

The replacement of the first group of chosen guests by those drawn from the roadways often has been read in a supersessionist way to suggest the "replacement" of the chosen people by the gentile church. Such a construal is seriously problematic on many levels, not the least of which is the ethical problem of how it has fostered anti-Semitism and hatred of the Jewish people. The Matthean community could never have conceived of

8. Compare the earlier fishnet parable (Matt 13:47–50), which has similar eschatological themes and depicts the final judgment dividing the good from the bad, casting the wicked into the "fiery furnace" (13:50).

such an interpretation, and their scribal evangelists would be appalled to think that their parable had been read in such a way. Rather, the parable fits with a long-standing prophetic tradition critiquing the "hardness of heart" of the chosen people, warning them to return to God. The image of calling those from the crossroads fits with the practice of Jesus reaching out to "tax collectors and sinners" rather than preaching to established religious leaders. In other words, this parable's image of the call being ignored or refused by one group and accepted by another has a long history in Israel's self-critique. The distinctive feature here is that the second group does not exactly fit expectations, although it has resonances with the later prophetic tradition about the inclusion of gentiles in God's call to Israel (e.g., Zeph 3:9–20).

The apocalyptic tenor of the parable is highlighted in the concluding "judgment" element involving the binding and ejection of the inappropriately attired guest. As a story, the incident seems capricious. The substitute guests have been brought from the crossroads with no advance notification. How could they be expected to be attired in wedding garments? However, when the story is understood as an allegory of the final eschatological banquet (which often is depicted as a wedding feast), this difficulty disappears. Rather than actual clothing, the "wedding garments" become the fruits of repentance, devotion to God, the works of righteousness—all the elements of Jesus's gospel of the *basileia*.

Roman Taxes (22:15–22)

The next vignette depicts some emissaries of the Pharisees and Herodians coming to "entrap" Jesus by getting him on the record concerning his attitudes toward the Roman Empire, especially on the question of Roman taxation. The scene is based on the Markan version (12:13–17), which features representatives of the Pharisees and Herodians, although GMatthew focuses on the role of the Pharisees—presumably because the Herodian party no longer exists in the postwar period when GMatthew is being written, whereas the Pharisee party seems to have survived and morphed into the rabbinic school identified with the area near Jamnia (Yavneh). This Pharisaic-rabbinic tradition poses a key alternative to the first-century Jesus movement, so GMatthew tends to highlight debates between Jesus and representatives of the Pharisees.[9]

9. Of the various "parties" within Judaism of Jesus's day, Jesus's teaching is closest

The emissaries demand a ruling on the Roman census tax (v. 17). The *fiscus Judaicus* (which would have been the tax in question at the time GMatthew was being written) was a punitive measure imposed in the aftermath of the failed revolt in 66–73 CE. A head tax on each Jewish male, those funds supported the Roman military in the region (about three legions) as well as construction and maintenance of the Roman temple of Jupiter Optimus Maximus, which replaced the destroyed Jewish temple in Jerusalem. Thus, this tax was a rather "in-your-face" move by the Romans to ensure that, each year, the Jews would be reminded that they had lost the war and now funded Roman efforts to suppress any future uprisings. The tax in force during Jesus's own lifetime, the *tributum capitis*, was required of every male non-Roman inhabitant of the region ages fourteen to sixty-five. Those monies were used to fund the Roman military and other governmental functions, but at least the funds did not support a pagan temple.[10] We cannot be sure which tax is the key concern of the Matthean audience, but presumably the *fiscus Judaicus* was a livelier issue for them. Jesus's own audience, on the other hand, would have been concerned with the *tributum capitis*.

Since these "head taxes" were imposed only on non-Romans—the few who held Roman citizenship were exempt—it amounted to tribute imposed by the conquering power and was therefore despised by Jews who resented the Roman presence in the "land of promise." In combination with the *tributum soli* real estate tax, these census taxes provided both the reminder of Roman power and the financial means for the empire to maintain and project that power. The real estate taxes were paid in crops, while the "head tax" was paid in Roman coinage.[11]

---

to that of the Pharisees, so the frequency of debates with that group fits the historical circumstances, whether or not individual conflict scenes in GMatthew are judged to be historically reliable.

10. Note that the question posed to Jesus has to do with "tribute" to Rome, not the half-shekel temple tax prescribed by Exod 30:13–14 to be paid by every Jewish male between the ages of twenty and fifty years old, which supported the Jewish temple in Jerusalem. This tribute also included a land tax, the *tributum soli*.

11. For a brief and accessible discussion of this scene, see Keddie, "Render unto Caesar."

Silver denarius, struck 14–37 CE. Courtesy of the American Numismatic Society.

Rather than directly answering the question posed to him, Jesus asks to see an example of the coin used to pay the tax. Rhetorically, this is a clever move to put his opponents on the defensive: If they agree with the tax, why ask Jesus about it? But, if they oppose the tax, why would they have Roman coinage at the ready? As can be seen in the image of this silver denarius, struck during the reign of Tiberius Caesar (the emperor during Jesus's ministry), the obverse side of the coins features the head of the Roman emperor, while the reverse depicts the seated goddess Roma; any Jew would know that these representations violated the biblical commandment proscribing graven images (e.g., Exod 20:4). In addition, the inscriptions on the coinage name the emperor as *pontifex maximus* (chief priest and divinely sanctioned mediator between the divine and human realms) and as son of the divine Augustus ("Son of God"). Using such coinage implied agreement with the claims on the currency, which even the least scrupulous Jew would view as idolatrous.

With Jesus sidestepping the initial question about payment of Roman tribute, one might anticipate a similar demur from direct confrontation of the claims on "the tribute coin" (v. 19), but such is not the case. The opponents show Jesus one of the coins, and he challenges them, "Whose image is this and whose inscription?" (v. 20). The opponents admit that both are Caesar's. Jesus retorts, "Then repay to Caesar what belongs to Caesar and to God what belongs to God" (v. 21). The verb for "repay" (*apodidōmi*) carries the sense of discharging an obligation; according to Roman law, tribute is "due," so return to Caesar what money comes from Caesar. Avoid Roman coinage altogether—a move that would undermine the imperial economy.

Furthermore, Jesus undercuts the claims of empire embedded in the coinage by affirming that his audience should render "to God what belongs to God." By setting Caesar and God in opposition to each other, Jesus rejects the coins' claim regarding the divinity of Caesar. The one true God created the entire universe. What could possibly *not* belong to God? This interchange is not merely an affirmation of the so-called "separation of church and state." Jesus's response provokes a number of deeper questions about the relationship between Israel, God, and the Roman overlords. The fact that Jesus himself does not carry one of the Roman tribute coins itself speaks volumes about his concern to remain faithful to the true God and avoid bending to the grinding pressure to relinquish such devotion in the face of the raw power of Rome. Although this conflict story provides no explicit mention of Jesus's fate, his challenge to the imperial claims to divinity certainly provides a hint of the coming conflict.

Preparing for the Final Days

What Is Resurrection? (22:23–33)

A group of Sadducees came to Jesus to challenge the belief in the resurrection—a doctrine that this party within Judaism rejected because it was not taught in the Torah. (Jesus did affirm the resurrection of the just, which puts him in agreement with the Pharisee party.) The Sadducees use an extreme example of levirate marriage to ridicule the concept, assuming that the resurrected life will follow exactly the same patterns as the present life, including the concept of ownership of a wife by her husband (v. 28).

Jesus's response to this challenge is rather harsh: "You are wrong because you know neither the scriptures nor the power of God" (v. 29). He challenges the opponents' assumption of the identity of the resurrected life with our present existence: "In the resurrection, they neither take nor are given in marriage, but are like the angels" (v. 30 AT). This has been construed to mean that sexual relationships are transcended. Perhaps, but it also repudiates men's ownership of women, whether "their" wives or other family members. This rejection of a husband's presumed ownership and control of "his" wife fits with Jesus's prior teaching against the male prerogative in divorce (Matt 19:3–10). There is no gendered hierarchy among the angels; all are equal before God. The resurrection eliminates the patriarchal control of relationships presumed by the questioners.

For the sake of the Sadducees, who insist on the primacy of Torah in doctrinal matters, Jesus quotes the divine voice in Exod 3:6: "I am the God of Abraham, the God of Isaac, and the God of Jacob . . . not the God of the dead but of the living" (Matt 22:32). Thus, the Torah does provide a basis for the doctrine of the resurrection.

The Greatest Commandment (22:34–40)

In another scene drawn from GMark, Jesus faces another set of challengers, this time a group of Pharisees. The vignette in Mark 12:28–34 presents a relatively amiable encounter between Jesus and a scribe who has a favorable attitude toward his teaching. The scenario in GMatthew looks more like the Pharisees are tag-teaming the Sadducees. Perhaps they are favorably impressed at having "heard that he had silenced the Sadducees" (Matt 22:34) and therefore want to see to what extent he agrees with them. The Matthean scribes frame the conversation as a "test" (v. 35), but that need not be read as hostile; the question of the "greatest commandment" was a matter of discussion among Jewish teachers of the first two centuries CE.

Jesus responds by quoting part of the Shema (see Deut 6:5), a prayer recited thrice daily by devout Jews. He follows that by naming a second "great commandment," to love the neighbor as oneself (Lev 19:18b). Jesus asserts, "On these two commandments hang all the Law and the Prophets" (Matt 22:40). Unlike in the Markan version of the scene, the Matthean narrator provides no indication of any response to Jesus's assertions.

David's Son (22:41–46)

GMatthew shifts to Jesus questioning the Pharisees about the identity of the messiah. While both agree that the messiah is "Son of David," Jesus poses a riddle about how then David can call the messiah "Lord" (see Ps 110:1). The Pharisees offer no response to this interpretive question. This short exchange suggests that, while Jesus is the Messiah (Matt 16:16) and Son of David (1:1; 9:27), he is a greater than David, who prophetically names him Lord (*Kyrios*) in this psalm.

Denouncing the Scribes and Pharisees (23:1–36)

The gospel now segues to a section of invective and lamentation, using material based in part on GMark and Q[12] but most of which is distinctive to GMatthew. The warnings against "the scribes and the Pharisees" accuse them of hypocrisy (23:3), predatory practices (v. 4), and hypocritically performing religiosity for public acclaim rather than from sincere devotion (vv. 5–7).

Verses 8–12 seem out of place in this series, since they are directed toward the disciples ("you" [v. 8]) rather than against the scribes and Pharisees who are the subject of the remainder of the passage. A tenuous connection to the desire for honor (v. 7) sets the stage for these warnings against the kind of *philotimia* (love of honor and adulation) that was endemic to Greco-Roman society. Jesus here repeatedly tells the disciples to abjure the pursuit of honor. They should repudiate the titles of rabbi, father (*patēr*), and master (*kathēgētos*) because all disciples are siblings, with one teacher, one heavenly father, and one master, the Messiah (vv. 8–10). All those who follow Jesus must reject "greatness" and embrace humility. The greatest must become the servant (*diakonos*) of all (v. 11). The promise of eschatological reversal (v. 12) is perhaps designed to soften the blow to the egos of those who would resist this call.

The topic then returns to the critique of behaviors of the scribes and Pharisees. A series of seven "woes" repeatedly accuses these religious leaders of being hypocrites.[13] They allegedly use their keys to the *basileia* to lock people out and prevent anyone entering (v. 13); they go to great lengths to attract one convert but make that person a "child of Gehenna" (v. 15); blind guides, they make ridiculous distinctions between valid or invalid vows (vv. 16–22); they pay tithes of even the smallest produce of the land but neglect the more important matters of divine law (v. 23); they ritually cleanse dishes but themselves "are full of plunder and self-indulgence" (v. 25); they appear righteous on the outside but inside are corrupt (vv. 26–27); they revere the prophets of old and adorn their tombs, yet they oppose present divinely sent messengers and thus act like the ancestors who murdered the prophets of old (vv. 29–31).

The narrative voice changes in 23:34 to the I formula typical of prophetic speech. The divine voice asserts what is being done even now:

12. Mark 12:38–39; Luke 11:37–52; 13:34–35.

13. Some manuscripts add an eighth woe (Matt 23:14) that repeats the one accusation in GMark about "devour[ing] widow's houses" (Mark 12:40).

"Behold, I send to you prophets and wise persons and scribes" (v. 34a AT). Rather than listening to these present emissaries, the divine voice predicts aggressive resistance: "Some of them you will kill and crucify, some of them you will scourge in your synagogues and pursue from town to town" (v. 34b). As a result, the guilt of shedding righteous blood will come upon "this generation" (vv. 35–36).

The hostility toward "scribes and Pharisees" in this section of GMatthew represents the conflicted environment of the post-resurrection period—perhaps especially the heated internecine disputes of the 50s–70s CE, leading up to, during, and after the First Jewish War—not the environment during the lifetime of Jesus himself. These denunciations are rhetorically charged, not historical reports of actual behaviors of Jewish teachers or the Pharisee party. The opponents' depiction represents a postwar review of events of the recent past; the predictions comprise prophecies *ex eventu*. The warnings fit with traditional Hebrew prophetic threats of judgment for Israel's disobedient behavior; they are neither unique to GMatthew nor particularly harsh in that context. Still, their placement in the gospel highlights the Matthean community's conflicted relationship with other Jewish groups of the 70s–80s CE.

Jesus Laments over Jerusalem (22:37–39)

Jesus's lament over Jerusalem resonates with the prophetic warnings in the previous I-formula speech. In this Q tradition (Luke 13:34–35), Jerusalem is personified as "you who kill the prophets and stone those sent to you" (v. 37a). Jesus desires "to gather your children together" under protective wings like a mother bird does with her brood (v. 37b; compare Pss 17:8; 91:4) but to no avail—the people refuse to gather to him. This sense of refusal anticipates future scenes in the gospel, especially the ultimate rejection of Jesus by the powers-that-be in Jerusalem who bring about his execution. As is typical with biblical laments, it ends with a warning of desolation for lack of response to the divine call (v. 38). The city's conversion is presented as an eschatological possibility (v. 39; 24:30), yet the Matthean audience would remember the city's destruction by Rome and perhaps be skeptical of its potential restoration.

Conclusions

This section of the gospel brings the teaching and ministry of Jesus to a sharper edge, highlighting the cost of discipleship. Jesus's teaching is not far from that of the Pharisees but is presented as both simpler and more demanding. Rather than developing rules about which vows are binding and which not, simply take all vows as binding (23:16–22). Rather than debating the validity of Roman tribute, avoid using Roman coinage altogether (22:15–22). Rather than parsing the rules about precisely when a husband can unilaterally dismiss his wife, reject the idea altogether (19:3–12) and eschew such patriarchal power structures (23:8–12). It is irrelevant to *talk* about obedience to God; what matters is *enacting* that obedience (21:28–32). God is generous and desires the wholeness of every human being, regardless of how long it takes that person to answer the divine call (20:1–16). Those who value wealth or power cannot enter the *basileia* (19:16–30; 20:20–28), an environment in which love of God and love of neighbor provide the entire grounds for communal existence (Matt 22:34–40)—rules that even non-lawyers can grasp and follow.

The series of vignettes depicting Jesus's ministry in Judea highlight the attempts of those in positions of power to control him and make his teaching fit their predetermined categories, but Jesus persistently challenges the categories themselves as exclusionary, exploitative, or otherwise wrongheaded. Those who dismiss the doctrine of the resurrection do so because they have "dumbed down" the meaning to make it ridiculous. But the resurrected life is "like the angels in heaven" (22:30), beyond human understanding in our present condition (22:29–33). Those in control of the Jerusalem temple have allowed it to be misused, a "den of brigands" rather than a house of prayer (21:12–17). The Matthean scribes take some leeway when presenting the story of Jesus after the fact, knowing what did in fact happen to Jesus once the political leaders became convinced he was a threat to their power and to the peace of Jerusalem. Nevertheless, the gospel of Jesus and his critique of those power structures unavoidably would lead to a serious clash at some point. Jesus's *basileia* teaching and praxis conflicted with the Roman *basileia* in the province of Judea, and that conflict could not perdure.

The next section of GMatthew uses apocalyptic language and imagery to reconfigure this human political conflict on the grand scale of the universal conflict of good and evil.

Review and Discussion Questions

A. Review Questions

1. In what ways does Jesus overturn a husband's right to divorce his wife?
2. What are some of the important features of the speech-act of Jesus "cleansing" the temple (Matt 21:12–17)? How does this scene show Jesus enacting the *basileia* message?
3. What are some of the key features of the scene where the Pharisees and Herodians question Jesus about paying taxes to the Roman Empire (Matt 22:15–22)?

B. Discussion Questions

1. What difference does it make if we view Jesus's teaching in Matt 19:3–12 as having to do with divorce in general terms versus the more specific terms of a husband's right to divorce his wife? Why might Jesus have been inclined to make that specific differentiation? Why would that distinction matter to a contemporary audience?
2. Some contemporary American Christians support posting the Ten Commandments in public buildings (e.g., schools, courthouses). Other US Christians criticize such initiatives, alleging that proponents do not live up to the two Great Commandments quoted by Jesus (e.g., Matt 22:34–40). Leaving aside the questions of religious freedom, public displays of religion, and that sort of thing, what really is at stake in the choice about preferring Jesus's Great Commandments versus the Ten Commandments? What image of God lies behind each choice?
3. When Jesus answers the Pharisees and Herodians about paying taxes to the Roman Empire (Matt 22:15–22), he undercuts the claims of every human empire and privileges the claims of the *basileia* of God. In what ways is this teaching important for contemporary disciples of Jesus?

Chapter 8

PREPARING FOR THE END-TIMES

The Eschatological Discourse (Matt 24–25)

THE MATTHEAN SCRIBES UNDERSTAND the *basileia* message as a call to change human relationships in the immediate context—personal, economic, and political—as well as a message of divine transformation of those relationships as God draws all of creation toward its final purpose and goal of reconciliation and justice. The scribal community reflected deeply on this concept and plumbed the depths of the Jewish Scriptures to find what they saw as the best ways to represent this theme. Their choice of apocalyptic language and imagery is apt in that it vividly presents the perennial conflict of good and evil. The very vividness of that imagery, however, poses a danger for modern readers not familiar with apocalyptic literature. We need to avoid uncritically adopting apocalypticism's we/they rhetoric and dualistic worldview.

This final discourse of the fifth book of GMatthew is called "eschatological" because it outlines the *eschata*, the "last things" marking the transformation of the world from its current sociopolitical realities to God's *basileia*, which throws those power structures on their head. The section initially (Matt 24:1—25:44) follows the "little apocalypse" of Mark 13 and then shifts to a combination of materials drawn from Q and the unique Matthean source M (Matt 24:45—25:46). The Matthean scribes have edited the materials in both sections to suit the needs of their particular community in the 80s CE, emphasizing vigilant endurance in discipleship while awaiting God's final judgment and the establishment of divine rule.

Calamities of the Final Days

While this section of GMatthew presents "predictions" of events that were to take place after Jesus's lifetime, at least some of those events were past history for the scribal evangelists. They follow the biblical prophets in presenting calamities that befall Israel as divine punishment for ignoring prophetic warnings and refusing to correct their disobedient ways. As is the case with the "woes" in Matt 23, these complaints exemplify the long-standing self-critique of the Israelite community, not anti-Jewish sentiments.

Destruction of the Temple (24:1–2)

Jesus predicts the destruction of the Jerusalem temple, using language reminiscent of the preexilic prophets. This brief reprise creates a connection between the "desolation" mentioned two verses earlier (23:38), tying it directly to the temple as the center point of the "house" of Israel. The threat of destruction is total, not one stone left upon another (24:2). Those who lived through the Roman conquest of Jerusalem in 70 CE could not possibly miss the connections.

Calamities Foretold (24:3–14)

Immediately after the renewed prediction of calamities, we see the disciples approach Jesus for a timeline: "Tell us, when will this happen, and what sign will there be of your coming, and of the end of the age?" (v. 4). Note that, while Jesus spoke of the parousia (appearance or coming) of the Human One as a future event, the disciples here identify Jesus as that coming figure. This suggests a post-resurrection context rather than a discussion that could have happened during Jesus's lifetime.

Jesus does not answer the request for a timeline for the parousia and final judgment (see also 24:36). Instead, he warns against premature decisions or support for false messiah figures (vv. 4–5). The Matthean Jesus presents a list of "signs" that must precede the end-time—wars, revolutions, earthquakes. These are birth pangs of the parousia (vv. 6–8) but not definitive evidence of the event itself. The Jewish revolt happened during the lifetime of members of the Matthean community, so they certainly had experienced the war and revolution part of this prediction. The gospel also mentions earthquakes at both the death and resurrection of Jesus

(27:51 and 28:2, respectively). Yet these events are not to be taken as indicating the imminent parousia.

In the Markan original, this prediction tells that earlier community of Christ believers that the war they were enduring was not a reliable sign of the end-time, and the Jewish generals being acclaimed as messiahs were among the false messiah figures mentioned in the prior verses. In the Matthean context, the warnings have less immediacy but perhaps more salience. "How long, O Lord?" is an implied subtheme to this request for a timeline. The voice of Jesus here is not incredibly reassuring.

The discussion turns to warnings of persecutions that will ensue for the disciples, anticipating that they will take the gospel to "all nations" (v. 9), as well as dangers that will arise within the community of believers itself. The voice warns of betrayals by fellow community members, deception by false prophets, members falling away because of loss of hope, the "love of many . . . [growing] cold" (vv. 10–12). These few verses are unique to GMatthew, so imply that such troubling details represent the current or recent experience of the Matthean community. Yet, hope is encouraged: Those who persevere to the end will be rescued (v. 13). Meanwhile, the gospel of the *basileia* must be preached "throughout the world as a witness to all nations" before the end will come (v. 14).

Great Tribulation (24:15–28)

This sequence of warnings reprises the major signs of the upheaval before the end-time: the "desolating abomination" that will be installed in the Jerusalem temple (v. 15), great tribulation that will incite immediate flight, regardless of Sabbath or winter weather (vv. 16–22).[1] The warning against false messiahs is repeated and expanded (vv. 23–28). For the first time in this gospel, the parousia of the eschatological figure known as the Human One is equated with the appearance of the Messiah. This conflation provides

1. Mark 13:14 depicts this flight as "to the mountains," although it is not clear precisely which mountains are in view. Following Eusebius Pamphilus, early tradition identified this flight as to Pella, a city in the Transjordan region. Eusebius indicates that such a flight did take place at the time of the First Jewish Revolt (*Church History* 3.5.3). It is unclear whether the Matthean scribes were aware of this specific tradition, since Eusebius was writing about two and a half centuries later.

The remark about hoping that the flight will not occur on the Sabbath is unique to GMatthew. The addition suggests that the Matthean community continued to observe the Jewish calendar and at least some of the Torah prohibitions incumbent upon devout Jews.

the basis for the later doctrine of the "second coming," which inherently identifies both figures with the risen Jesus.

The Coming of the Human One (24:29–31)

The parousia of the Human One is said to come "immediately" after the events of the tribulation (v. 29)—a detail again unique to GMatthew.[2] Oddly, this Matthean addition makes the prediction patently false, since the tribulations associated with the war already have happened in the recent past of the Matthean community. Some interpreters have suggested the use of the term here conveys not a time frame but rather the surety that the parousia will take place.[3] Such a reassurance certainly would be helpful to the Matthean community as they deal with the emotional fallout from a seven-year war that ended barely a decade before this gospel was completed.

The description of the parousia of the Human One derives its main figure from the prophecy of Dan 7:13, while other details are drawn from Isa 13:10, 13 (the cosmic signs); Zech 12:12–14 (the mourning of the nations); and Isa 27:13 (the trumpet blast). The gathering of the chosen "from the four winds" (v. 31) harkens back to the requirement that the gospel be spread to all the nations (v. 14) and presumes that peoples from all across the earth will have heard and responded to the call of the God of Israel (Isa 61:11).

Parables and Figures of the Final Days

The Fig Tree (24:32–35)

The image of the fig tree provides an alternative response to the question of "when" all these things will happen. Seeing "these signs" (presumably, the tribulations previously outlined) will indicate for the audience that the parousia is "near," the Human One "at the very gates" (v. 33). The quote in v. 34, "Truly I tell you, this generation will not pass away until all these things have taken place," repeats Mark 13:30 but originally derives from Jesus himself.

2. Compare to Mark 13:24, which instead uses the relatively vague expression "in those days."

3. Another alternative would be that these predictions do indeed derive from the historical teaching of Jesus himself, who was mistaken in the timeline; GMark then would have removed the word "immediately" to eliminate the conflict between Jesus's words and the historical facts.

Both GMark and the Matthean scribes have reported it faithfully, even though they know that Jesus was mistaken in this detail. Not only his own generation but their immediate descendants would have died by the time GMatthew was being written. Perhaps to counter this rather embarrassing mistake, the gospel assures the audience that "heaven and earth will perish, but [Jesus's] words will not pass away" (v. 35; Mark 13:31).

The Unknown Hour (24:36–44)

The text goes on to confirm that the "hour" of the parousia cannot be calculated, for God alone knows when it will take place. God has not revealed this to anyone, not the angels, not even the Messiah (v. 36). It will come suddenly, when least expected, as suddenly as the flood in the days of Noah (vv. 37–39). One might be in the middle of a day's work, tilling a field or grinding at the mill when it happens (vv. 40–41).[4] The danger of lack of vigilance is highlighted in the image of the parousia as equivalent to a thief breaking and entering in the night to ravage a home and its inhabitants (v. 43).[5] There will be no advance warning; one must be prepared at every moment (v. 42–44).

Fate of Faithful and Unfaithful Servants (24:45–51)

This parable, drawn from the Q collection (Luke 12:41–46), highlights the particular importance of vigilance on the part of community leaders (the "servants" in the story). Those who are faithful are prepared for the master (*kyrios*) to return at any moment; being found obediently performing their assigned duties, they will be rewarded with promotion (vv. 45–47). Those who are not faithful will find themselves caught off guard, not only ignoring their appointed duties but abusing their fellow servants; they will be flogged so severely they are cut in two and then will be cast out with the hypocrites (vv. 48–51).

4. It may be worth noting that the use of these two verses to support a doctrine known as the rapture was a late nineteenth-century innovation. The text here depicts an abbreviated last judgment scenario, not some purported ascension of individuals before the parousia and final judgment.

5. This image very likely goes back to Jesus himself, for it appears not only here but also in the earliest of the letters of Paul (1 Thess 5:2) and in the noncanonical Gos. Thom. 21; see also Gos. Thom. 103.

An interesting feature of this parable is the designated duty of the servants: "to give the other slaves their allowance of food at the proper time" (v. 45). The faithless servants are depicted as not only beginning to beat their fellow servants but also to "eat and drink with drunkards" (v. 49), thereby depleting the household food stores and leaving the other household members to go hungry. We do not know the precise organization of the Matthean community, but these details suggest that shared meals and communal food stores were among its signature features.

Ten Maidens (25:1–13)

The story of the ten maidens, like other stories drawn from the M source, functions more as an allegory than a parable. The setting is the time of fulfillment of the *basileia* (v. 1). The wedding feast is prepared and all has been made ready for the arrival of the bridegroom, yet the bridal party does not know the exact time of his arrival.[6] Ten bridesmaids wait outside the gates, oil lamps at the ready, so they can light the groom's way as he processes toward the bridal pavilion. He is delayed. The sun sets and they must light their lamps to ensure the groom sees where they await him. Hours pass and they doze at their post, lamps burning all the while (v. 5). Half the group has brought extra flasks of oil; the other half came unprepared for such a long delay (vv. 2–4). Midnight strikes and someone spies the bridegroom; the maidens trim their lamps to ensure they burn brightly (vv. 6–7). Now the foolish maidens are revealed: Their lamps sputter for lack of oil and soon will be extinguished. They ask the wise maidens to share some of their supply but are rebuked and given the impossible task of going to the market at midnight to buy additional oil (vv. 8–9). The foolish maidens follow this ridiculous advice, and the groom arrives during their absence. The wise maidens enter the wedding feast with him, but the foolish ones are locked out (v. 10). When they arrive late—whether their shopping expedition was successful or not, we are not told, since by now it is irrelevant—the doorkeeper refuses admission; the householder (the *kyrios*) rejects them utterly, disclaiming any knowledge of them (vv. 11–12). The narrator concludes with a reminder to be vigilant, since no one knows the precise time of the parousia.

6. The scenario fits that of a monarch's marriage, where a distance must be traveled from one realm to another, although typically a royal bride would be taken to the king's realm rather than the matrilocal marriage imaged here. Perhaps this detail of the story is intended to hint at Gen 2:24, which presents matrilocal marriage as the pre-fall ideal.

The Matthean community certainly identifies the parable's bridegroom with Jesus, whom they also identify as the eschatological Human One who will complete the establishment of God's *basileia* at the glorious parousia. As in the earlier story of the wedding feast (Matt 22:1–14), the *basileia* is depicted as a festal banquet uniting God with the chosen people. Following the tradition of the Hebrew prophets, that unity is modeled after the most intimate of human bonds, the marital relationship.[7]

This particular story does not focus on the marriage itself but rather on the wedding feast, a time of merriment for all those involved. Wedding banquets celebrate the merger of families, provide ample food and drink for all the guests, and allow time for rest and relaxation, like an extended Sabbath. This image of rest and festival, highlighted in this parable, fund the audience's imagination about what the anticipated *basileia* will be like (compare to Isa 25:6–9). If one must be ready for its approach at any moment, this vision provides ample incentive to do so.[8]

Ten Talents (25:14–30)

The parable of the talents, which derives from the Q tradition (Luke 19:12–27), repeats the theme of vigilance but also highlights accountability, reinforcing the message of the previous Q parable of the faithful and unfaithful servants (Matt 24:45–51). Since the talent is a unit of ancient currency, this parable has more explicit economic dynamics than the prior one.

7. As scholars have pointed out since at least the 1960s, the marriage metaphor is fraught with difficulties when taken too far. E.g., the metaphor in Ezek 16, which presumes a patriarchal model of marriage, takes on quite abusive traits and presents violence against women/wives as divinely sanctioned—implicitly supporting a heinous ethical standpoint. The application of the metaphor to Christ and the church requires men in the church to view themselves as the feminine partner—at best an awkward position for straight men—and implicitly sexualizes women's relationship with Christ. For a brief discussion of some of these difficulties, see Macwilliam, "Marriage Metaphors in Prophets."

8. Compare to James Charlesworth and Loren Stuckenbruck's discussion of the Qumran text 1Q28a, the Rule of the Congregation (also known as the Messianic Rule), which outlines community activities, including their meals, carried out in the expectation of the imminent arrival of the final days. Like the Matthean community approximately 150 years later, "each feast was an enactment of what the messianic banquet would be like" (Charlesworth and Stuckenbruck, "Rule of the Congregation," 108). Both the wedding feast image and the Last Supper institution narrative follow the same basic theological perspective as that in this first-century BCE Messianic Rule.

A person preparing for a journey delegated financial responsibilities to three slaves, who seem to have functioned as stewards for the household. The investor entrusted three allotments of the estate to the three stewards, in disproportionate divisions of five, two, and one talent, each according to the investor's judgment of the steward's skill (25:14–15). Given that one silver talent was the equivalent of six thousand denarii—roughly twenty years' wages—even the least of the stewards was delegated an enormous sum of money to invest—approximately $1,000,000. Upon the departure of the investor, the first two stewards immediately put their resources to work, trading with the funds and doubling their value (vv. 16–17). The third steward took an easier route, avoiding risk and involving little labor: this one dug a hole, hid the money in the ground (v. 18), and went back home to sit and do nothing.

After a long absence, the investor returns to settle accounts (v. 19). The first two stewards come forward with their reports of investments and earnings, are lauded by the investor for their success, and are welcomed to "enter into the joy of your master [*kyrios*]" (vv. 20–23). The last steward, in a report ridden with insults to deflect the blame of inaction onto the investor, admits to having hidden the remaining talent out of fear of reprisal if the money were lost (vv. 24–25). The investor rebukes this last steward as wicked and lazy, using a sly rhetorical riposte to suggest that the insults about past behaviors should have prompted at least a safe investment like a bank deposit, where the funds would have earned a modicum of interest (vv. 26–27). Instead, the steward showed utter incompetence and sloth.

As a result, the investor orders the one talent handed over to the first steward (v. 28), while the lazy steward is cast into the outer darkness (v. 30). The maxim in v. 29 (compare Matt 13:12)—essentially equivalent to the proverb· "The rich get richer, and the poor get poorer"—justifies the rewards and punishment depicted at the dénouement of the story but should not be taken as indicative of Jesus's own economic ideal. It may be an accurate statement of how economies work, but it contradicts Jesus's teaching about distribution of wealth elsewhere in the gospel. The more pertinent message of the parable involves the demand for accountability when the *Kyrios* returns.

The Last Judgment

Judgment of the Nations (25:31–46)

This last segment of the Matthean eschatological discourse depicts the parousia of the Human One, immediately followed by the final judgment of all the nations, the gospel by then having been preached throughout the world (25:31–32; see also 24:14). Using the image of a shepherd who divides the flock, the scene depicts the just as "sheep" and the sinister as "goats" (v. 33). The just are welcomed into the *basileia*, while the unjust are relegated to eternal torment (vv. 34, 41, 46).[9]

It is worth emphasizing that the sole grounds for judgment here comprise a set of specific observable behaviors towards others: feeding the hungry, giving drink to the thirsty, welcoming the stranger, clothing the naked, caring for the sick, and visiting the imprisoned (vv. 34–36, 42–43). The *sola fides* slogan of Martin Luther, at least as it typically is construed in contemporary Christian circles, does not do justice to this Matthean perspective. There is no question of "faith" in the sense of affirmation of particular credal statements, not even ones concerning Jesus. GMatthew falls more in line with the view in the Epistle of James, that "faith" concerns behaviors, not intellectual assertions (e.g., Jas 2:18). The specific actions listed as the grounds for judgment have since become codified as "the corporal works of mercy."[10]

Both the just and the sinister are depicted as surprised at the judgment: "When was it that we saw you . . .?" (vv. 37–39, 44). But the judge affirms, "Just as you did [or did not do] to one of these least . . ., you did [or did not do] to me" (vv. 40, 45; compare 10:42). The judgment is based on faithfulness, concrete behaviors that demonstrate one's commitment to discipleship, following the way of Jesus in community relations and in relations with every other person with whom the disciple comes into contact, for every individual has the face of Messiah Jesus.

9. The concept of eternal punishment has received serious criticism in the last century of interpretation, for solid theological reasons. While punishment of the wicked seems to serve the needs of retributive justice, the notion of eternal punishment seems to turn God into a terribly vindictive judge, utterly unlike the Abba God revealed by Jesus. Suffice it to say that this view of eternal punishment is not unique to GMatthew but appears in other Jewish and Christian literature both before and after this gospel (e.g., Ps 140:10; Rev 19:20; 20:10; 1 En. 10:13).

10. The tradition adds burying the dead as a seventh corporal work of mercy. For more information, see USCCB, "Corporal Works of Mercy."

End of GMatthew Book 5 (26:1a)

This fifth "book of Jesus" again concludes with the formula "When Jesus had finished saying all these things . . ." (Matt 26:1a). Appropriately enough, given the topic of the eschatological discourse, this is the last appearance of the formula in GMatthew. The gospel next turns to the narrative of the arrest, trial, execution, death, and resurrection of Jesus.

Conclusions

Book 5 of Jesus in GMatthew highlights what twentieth-century German theologian Dietrich Bonhoeffer called "the cost of discipleship."[11] The parables and allegories included in this fifth book repeatedly emphasize the faithfulness and vigilance required of the disciples of Jesus as they await the parousia and fulfillment of the *basileia* he inaugurated (24:45—25:30). The question of *when* this fulfillment will take place is deflected as abstruse knowledge belonging to God alone, but the traditional apocalyptic calamities are listed as precursor warning signs (24:1–44). The significance of faithfulness is affirmed in the last judgment scene, which heightens the demand by affirming the eternity of both the reward and the punishment due to the just and unjust (25:31–46). Specific behavioral standards are set forth as the basis for this judgment; none of the criteria concern credal statements of any kind. The final judgment scene presumes the gospel has been spread to the entire world, Jews and gentiles alike, but *cognitive* acceptance of the gospel is not a criterion for judgment; *following* the gospel and imitating the example of Jesus provide the sole foundation for the divine judge's discernment between the just and the unjust. Nor is there any excuse for not behaving justly, since the list of behaviors is quite succinct, and everyone who comes into someone's orbit of experience provides the opportunity for treating them as one would Christ Jesus.

Review and Discussion Questions

A. Review Questions

1. What are some of the "costs of discipleship" according to GMatthew?

11. Bonhoeffer, *Cost of Discipleship*.

2. In the last judgment scene (Matt 25:31–46), what criteria are used to count someone among the righteous (the sheep) versus the unjust (the goats)?
3. This section of GMatthew focuses attention on the "end-time," that is, the final period before the parousia and fulfillment of the *basileia*. Various calamities are presented as "signs of the times" and warnings of the coming judgment. What are some of the key elements of this series of warnings?

B. Discussion Questions

1. The last judgment scene in Matt 25:31–46 depicts eternal rewards for the just and eternal punishment for the unjust. At least since the twentieth century, the notion of eternal punishment has been challenged as a theological contradiction of the God of love and mercy taught elsewhere in the Bible and inherent in the gospel of Jesus. What do you think about that? Is eternal punishment unfitting for the God of mercy revealed in Jesus? How so or how not?
2. Unlike what many see in the letters of Paul (e.g., Rom 10:9), GMatthew never stipulates belief in Jesus as required for eternal reward. Specific behavioral standards—not credal statements—are set forth as the basis for God's judgment of the individual at the end-time. Yet there are groups today who claim to be Christian yet totally reverse the emphasis of the Matthean scribes: Credal statements are everything; "believers" can engage in all sorts of avaricious and immoral behaviors while still claiming to "be saved" (e.g., churches that follow the so-called "gospel of wealth"). What do you make of this disparity?
3. Why do you think the Matthean scribes include warnings of the coming judgment as we near the end of their gospel? What purpose did those predictions serve for the original audience? Do they still function that way for a contemporary audience? How so or how not?

Chapter 9
THE PASSION AND RESURRECTION NARRATIVES
(Matt 26–28)

Conspiracy, Preparation, Betrayal

THROUGHOUT THE PASSION NARRATIVE, the Matthean scribes essentially follow the Markan story, with slight modifications that will be noted as we go through the text.

The Conspiracy Begins (26:1–5)

The scene begins with Jesus reminding the disciples of the calendar: Passover is in two days. The Matthean scribes take the opportunity to turn this reminder into a final prediction of the passion: Passover is coming, "and the Human One will be handed over to be crucified" (26:2 AT). The text clearly refers to Jesus, but the use of the title here reinforces the earlier claims that identify Jesus as Messiah and the eschatological Human One. The religious leaders in Jerusalem meet in private, at the villa of Joseph ben Caiaphas, the high priest at that time (18–36 CE). They deliberate how to arrest Jesus and put him to death but are wary of taking action during the Passover Festival for fear the people will riot (vv. 2–5).

The concern about the people rioting would derive from two factors, the sheer number of pilgrims in Jerusalem for this festival—a mandatory pilgrimage feast (see Deut 16:16)—and the liberation theme of the festival. Passover commemorates the Israelites' escape from enslavement in Egypt and the subsequent gift of their safe return to the promised land. By speaking of God's *basileia*, Jesus controverted the authority of Rome in the land of Israel. To arrest him would make the religious leaders appear to be on the side of Rome against the God of Israel—a dynamic virtually guaranteed to provoke riots.

Yet, the remark about avoiding the festival remains anomalous. Passover is a weeklong celebration, and the reminder in v. 2 indicates that it will begin in two days. The arrest of Jesus is not situated ten days later, after the festival was over. Rather, the narrative indicates in fact it took place toward the beginning of the Passover feast (on Nisan 14), hard on the heels of the opening Seder celebration. And there is no mention of riots at any point. The historical record seems muddled, but we do not have sufficient information to correct any of the details. The timeline and warning both are part of the narrative in GMark, so the Matthean scribes simply reused this inherited tradition.

Anointing at Bethany (26:6–13)

The anointing scene is a fraught passage to discuss, not because the scene itself is difficult, but because of what is called its reception history, that is, the history of the discussion and artistic presentations of this scene over time. For example, nearly every life-of-Jesus movie has turned this story into an oversexed scene with the woman portrayed as a prostitute (or, at best, a courtesan). None of those features applies to the gospel stories of this scene, unless one really stretches the details from GLuke. GMatthew follows the Markan version of the vignette almost verbatim (Mark 14:3–9); in both cases, we see a woman prophet engaged in honorable behavior and herself deserving of respect.

The scene takes place at the household of "Simon the leper" (presumably the *former* leper) in Bethany, about an hour's walk from Jerusalem (v. 6). The guests are reclining at table, following the Greco-Roman customs of the time. A woman brings an alabaster jar of perfumed oil and pours it on Jesus's head (v. 7). This is a speech-act prophecy marking Jesus as the "anointed one" (Messiah). GMatthew does not give this woman prophet a speaking role but, for a scribal community that knows the whole history of Israel, the act itself tells all. Whereas GMark says that "some" protested this prophetic act, calling it a waste, GMatthew attributes the protest to the Twelve themselves

(v. 8). Shockingly, this implies that they reject the woman's identification of Jesus as the Messiah, in spite of their long travels with him from Galilee to this little town near Jerusalem. Their purported reason for objecting is that the perfumed oil was valuable and could have been sold to benefit the poor (v. 9), but how could it be a "waste" to identify the true Messiah and symbolically proclaim him before the people of Israel? The true reason for their rejection is hidden from view, but the story implies that the Twelve are not convinced that Jesus is the promised Messiah-King.

Jesus rebukes their challenge of the woman, silencing their complaints and affirming that "she has done a beautiful work for me" (v. 10 NABRE). He adds interpretive words to her silent speech-act. Jesus will not always be with them. Unlike these twelve male disciples, she realizes Jesus's messianic role soon will end in death, so she has anointed his body for burial (v. 11–12). Simon Peter might have affirmed the messianic identity of Jesus in an earlier scene (16:16), but he still does not understand that reality from God's point of view (16:22–23). Only the prophetic woman here realizes what that messianic role will demand of Jesus.

In response to her symbolic proclamation, Jesus solemnly promises: "Truly I tell you, wherever this good news is proclaimed in the whole world, what she has done will be told in remembrance of her" (v. 13). All four canonical gospels have an anointing story, so the early churches did their part to try to fulfill this promise of Jesus. Unfortunately, the later tradition has discouraged the remembrance that Jesus wanted to preserve.

Judas Sells Out (26:14–16)

Judas Iscariot goes to the "chief priests" to see what they will give him to hand Jesus over to them (vv. 14–15a). This is an odd use of the plural since, according to Torah, only one chief priest serves at a given time (e.g., Exod 28:1–2; 29:4–5). Perhaps the narrator means the group of elder priests, including Caiaphas, the high priest. While all the canonical gospels depict this Judas as betraying Jesus, only GMatthew implies that the move was driven by avarice.

The priests accept the offer from Judas and set a price of thirty pieces of silver as a reward—a rather modest amount equivalent to about a month's wages. This amount would prompt Jewish members of the audience to remember Torah legislation concerning recompense for physical injuries (e.g., Exod 21:32, the compensation paid to someone whose slave has been gored by an ox) and severance pay to a rejected shepherd when the covenant was abrogated (Zech 11:10–14). The symbolism of the Zechariah text, featuring an abrogated covenant and dismissed shepherd, seems theologically the most apt to this particular case.

Passover Preparations (26:17–19)

Judas's behavior behind the scenes has not yet come to the attention of Jesus or the remaining disciples. Instead, they are focused on the rapidly approaching festival. GMatthew uses "Unleavened Bread" and "Passover" language to refer to the same feast; although they began in ancient Israel as two independent festivals, one having to do with the spring harvest and another with lambing season, gradually the two were merged because they fell close to the same time of year.[1]

The disciples ask Jesus where he wants to celebrate the Passover—a reasonable question since there is no evidence that he has a residence in Jerusalem (v. 17). Jesus tells them to go to "a certain person" in the city and give him a prearranged message from "the Teacher," saying that "my time" (*kairos*) has drawn near (v. 18).[2] This individual clearly was a disciple of Jesus, although GMatthew does not so identify the person. Once the disciples have identified the correct individual, they prepare the Passover at that house. Because the Matthean scribes retain their historically false equation of "the disciples" with the Twelve, the audience is led to believe that these twelve men did all the cooking, cleaning, and other preparations necessary for the Passover feast. In fact, the disciples were a mixed group of women and men, and numbered significantly more than twelve. Whether there were gendered role divisions among them is unknown but certainly should not be assumed.

1. For the connection between the two festivals, see, e.g., Exod 12:3–20; 34:18; Lev 23:4–8; Num 9:2–14; 28:16–17; Deut 16:1–8. The Passover, commemorating the redemption from enslavement in Egypt, began at sundown after the Passover lamb was sacrificed in the Jerusalem temple on the afternoon of 14 Nisan. The eating of unleavened bread was connected with the Passover Seder, since the enslaved Israelites had to flee suddenly to make their escape from Egypt. The use of unleavened bread and a sacrificial lamb for Passover provided the symbolic grounds for merger of the two festivals. By Jesus's time, the feast continued through 21 Nisan.

2. This coded-message scenario modifies the version in Mark 14:13–16, which tells the disciples to look for their target based on the countercultural behavior of a man carrying a water jar. The Matthean version implies somewhat more foresight and advance coordination on Jesus's part.

The Fate of the Betrayer (26:20–25)

Jesus and the Twelve recline at table to celebrate the Passover Seder (v. 20). Although it often has been assumed in the history of interpretation of this scene, and has been codified in such artistic presentations as that of Leonardo da Vinci, there are no grounds for the assumption that these thirteen named men were the *only* persons present at the meal. In fact, given the role divisions for a Seder, it is virtually impossible to celebrate the feast without a mixed familial group that includes women and children. The Twelve are identified here not because they were the only group present but because they were the ones on the proverbial hot seat. Jesus's other disciples are guiltless; the betrayer will come from among the Twelve (v. 21). Each of the men acts shocked at this revelation and refuses to admit he is the one (v. 22), but Jesus affirms that the betrayer will be among those who have eaten from the common dish with him (v. 23; compare Ps 41:10)—a heinous violation of the laws of hospitality. The narrator asserts that, even though this fulfills the predetermined fate of the Human One, it would be better for the betrayer to have never been born (v. 24). At this point, Judas interjects the half-hearted assertion framed as an interrogative: "Surely, it is not I, Rabbi?" To which Jesus replies, "You yourself have said it" (v. 25 NABRE). The scene thus affirms Jesus's betrayal by one of his most intimate companions—a horrific act of treachery. Yet Jesus was not duped. He realized what was happening but remained faithful to what God had called him to do.

The Last Supper (26:26–30)

The narrative of the Last Supper appears in two different versions in the New Testament. The earliest is that of Paul, which is followed by GLuke (1 Cor 11:23–25; Luke 22:19–20); the other is that of GMark, which is followed here by GMatthew (Mark 14:22–26). Another early Christian text contemporaneous with the canonical gospels, the Teaching of the Twelve Apostles (typically shortened to Didache), presents the earliest eucharistic prayer, but without a formal "institution narrative" recalling what Jesus did at his last meal with the disciples. While the Synoptic Gospels present the Last Supper as a Passover Seder meal, the prayer in Did. 9 is the only version that presents the blessing on the cup first and then the bread, following the order designated for the Seder.

Blessings over the food are customary for devout Jews at every meal. The blessing over bread (*hamotzi*) covers all types of food except wine, which has a separate blessing. What we see in the narrative of the Last Supper is Jesus pronouncing a blessing over all the food; the two blessings over bread and wine are all inclusive.

The distinctive feature of the Last Supper, of course, is the innovative interpretation Jesus gives to the bread and wine at this meal. The bread of flight and liberation becomes his body, while the wine of joy in the promised land becomes his blood. The Matthean scribes add the interpretive comment that this "blood of the covenant . . . will be poured out on the many for the forgiveness of sins" (26:28 NABRE). The image of blood being shed *onto* someone alludes to the covenanting ceremony in Exod 24:8, where Moses sprinkles the blood of the sacrificial animals on the people of Israel gathered at Mount Sinai. The nation has just heard the full proclamation of divine law and has affirmed that "everything the Lord has said we will do" (Exod 24:3). This covenantal blood seals their promise and affirms that they have put their lives on the line to fulfill this commitment. Now it is Jesus's blood that seals the disciples to this renewed covenant with the God of Israel, whose *basileia* is being inaugurated in the community of those who share this covenantal meal.

In Jesus's reinterpretation of this covenanting scene, "the many" refers to all Israel—not simply "many," as if some are excluded. The later use of this language by the Matthean scribes extends its meaning to all people, gentiles included. The Matthean community already includes gentile converts to the Jesus movement and, as we have seen before, the narrative anticipates the gospel being preached to all the nations before the end-time (e.g., 24:14).

As their meal finishes, Jesus tells the disciples that "I will never again drink of this fruit of the vine until that day when I drink it new with you in my Father's kingdom" (v. 29). This implies that Jesus himself saw the fulfillment of the *basileia* coming very soon, certainly within the lifetime of his initial disciples (24:34). The scene concludes with them singing a hymn—presumably one or more of the thanksgiving songs in Pss 114–18 that conclude the Passover meal—and going to the Mount of Olives, east of Jerusalem across the Kidron Valley.

Peter's Betrayal Foretold (26:31–35)

Arriving on Mount Olivet, the narrative has Jesus predict that all the Twelve (not only Judas) will desert him at some point that night (v. 31; paraphrasing Zech 13:7). The prediction continues, "But after I am raised up, I will go ahead of you to Galilee" (v. 32). Note that, again, Jesus is the passive recipient of this raising; Jesus is the object of this miraculous work of God's restoration of the just. The detail about Jesus preceding them to Galilee provides the grounds for post-resurrection appearances of Jesus and also for the post-resurrection church taking root in Jesus's home territory.

Simon Peter acts in character to the way the gospel has portrayed him thus far: He brashly asserts that, whatever the others do, he will not abandon Jesus when the crunch comes (v. 33). Similarly to the earlier episode set in Caesarea Philippi (16:16, 21–23), Jesus rebukes Peter for his hubris and reinforces the prediction of betrayal. Indeed, before the end of the third watch of the night (twelve to three a.m., "cockcrow"), Peter will deny not merely once but three times (v. 34). Three is a perfect number in the Bible, so a threefold denial constitutes an ultimate and definitive repudiation. Peter continues to sputter protestations, including an avowal of willingness to die with Jesus, and is joined by the rest of the Twelve in these florid promises (v. 35). The audience, of course knows better. Jesus was right about their fickleness.

Agony in Gethsemane (26:36–46)

Jesus and the disciples move to an olive orchard on the western slope of the Mount of Olives, an area called Gethsemane, which means "oil press" (v. 36). GJohn calls it a "garden," although the Synoptic Gospels do not use this language. Jesus goes apart to pray, taking Peter, James, and John with him (v. 37). Asking the three to "keep watch with me," the narrator says Jesus prostrated himself in prayer, beseeching God to "let this cup pass from me; yet, not as I will, but as you will" (vv. 38–39 NABRE). Jesus returns to the three disciples, who are not watching but asleep. He rebukes them for their lack of vigilance and repeats his command to watch (vv. 40–41). This scenario is thrice repeated (vv. 42–45) until finally Jesus sees the betrayer coming (v. 46). The same disciples who swore they would not abandon Jesus, even on pain of death, have shown how hollow were those protestations. They could not even be bothered to stay awake for a few hours and support Jesus in prayer. This does not bode well for the ensuing scenes.

Betrayal and Arrest (26:47–56)

As Jesus is speaking, Judas Iscariot arrives on the scene, accompanied by an armed throng sponsored by "the chief priests and the elders of the people" (v. 47). The very leaders who were concerned to *avoid* arresting Jesus during the Passover for fear of a riot (26:5) are depicted as having changed strategy and enlisted the mob against him. Judas hails Jesus as "Rabbi"—the only disciple in GMatthew to use that title for Jesus—kissing him (v. 49). Oddly, the narrator characterizes this as a prearranged signal to show the officials which person to arrest (v. 48). It is difficult to imagine how antagonism against Jesus could have reached such a pitch without his opponents being able to recognize him on sight, especially because of the scenes of him preaching in public places like the temple. More likely, the narrator has included this interaction between Judas and Jesus to show the depth of the disciple's duplicity.

The narrator has Jesus respond to Judas with a curt remark equivalent to "Get on with it" and the mob roughly seizes Jesus (v. 50). One of the other disciples resists, drawing a short sword (a *machaira*, similar to a machete) and attacking the high priest's slave, cutting off his ear (v. 51). This is the first indication that any of the disciples were armed—and, make no mistake, the *machaira* is not a mere eating utensil but a warrior's blade designed to do precisely what is narrated here and more, to lop off the enemies' limbs. The historical probability of this taking place without starting a riot with dozens of people injured and all the disciples being arrested is virtually nil. However, the scene provides the narrator with the opportunity to put Jesus on record as opposed to armed rebellion (vv. 52–54).

The narrator presents Jesus as confronting the crowd: "Have you come out with swords and clubs to arrest me as though I were a rebel? Day after day I sat in the temple teaching, and you did not arrest me" (v. 55). The text continues by asserting that "all this" fulfills prophecy, although without specifying precisely which prophecies might be in view. The scene concludes with a note that the disciples forsook Jesus and fled the scene (v. 56), thereby proving Jesus's earlier prediction that the Twelve would all abandon him.

This mob scene in a dark and deserted place serves to raise the emotional level of the audience as they listen to the story of Jesus. The religious leaders' show of force in the middle of the night is ridiculous and craven. They could have apprehended Jesus in broad daylight, in the most public of places, the temple itself, at any point in the past several days—but, of course, then they would have been accountable to the crowds who were listening to Jesus and who might have been effective in preventing his arrest.

The story is designed throughout to convey that Jesus's arrest, trial, and execution were rigged, done at night, on the outskirts of town, with sham hearings behind closed doors and then in front of a mob that had been seeded with agents of powerful opponents who framed Jesus. GMatthew follows the Markan narrative throughout, so the Matthean scribes have not created this storyline nor constructed this adverse portrayal of the religious leaders working in the dark and abusing their power to suit their selfish purposes. By reusing the Markan material, they reinforce the image of Jesus's enemies as crafty and devious opponents of the truth.

The Trials of Jesus

Legally speaking, Jesus had one trial before the Roman official in charge of the province of Judea—in this case, Pontius Pilate, a Roman citizen of equestrian rank who served as prefect of Judea in 26–36 CE, under the emperor Tiberius (who reigned 14–37 CE). Sometimes the historical sources call Pilate a proconsul (e.g., the Roman historian Tacitus, writing about a century later), but his official title was prefect. The prefecture was a military appointment, but Pilate's responsibilities went beyond merely military concerns. Functionally, he was governor of the province, which meant he served as the high court judge for legal affairs in that region. Only the emperor could overrule his decisions, and only Roman citizens had the right to such an appeal. Jesus, of course, was not a Roman citizen, so had no right of appeal.

The Hearing Before the Sanhedrin (26:57–68)

The Matthean scribes follow Mark 14:53–65 in presenting the nighttime appearance of Jesus before the Sanhedrin as a trial, but this is not accurate to the historical circumstances. There were times in the first century when the prefecture was vacant and the Sanhedrin managed to function as the high court for the region (e.g., under Herod Agrippa I in 41–44 CE), but these were rare exceptions to the rule. "Sanhedrin" is a form of the Greek word *synedrion*, which means town council. Because of the Roman occupation of Judea, the Jerusalem *synedrion* did not have authority over the region; it had moral authority in matters of religion and could make recommendations to the Roman authorities about other concerns. Thus, although the narrative makes this session look like a trial, the better modern category would be that of a grand jury, which reviews evidence in a case to determine whether sufficient grounds exist to warrant going to trial.

The hearing is presented as taking place at night, and not just any night but the first evening of the Passover Festival. Either detail would be problematic, but the combination is outrageous. Work is forbidden on the first and last days of Passover; and, following the creation account in Gen 1, days are counted from sunset to sunset. The Sanhedrin would never have held a hearing on the first night of Passover. The narrative presents the timeline this way for two reasons: to reinforce that Jesus's arrest and condemnation were rigged, and to present the members of the Sanhedrin as hypocrites who would go to any lengths to see the end of Jesus. Following GMark, the Matthean scribes contend that Jesus himself was not guilty of any crimes, but his enemies did not care about justice. They wanted to prevent potential reprisals from Rome and were willing to sacrifice even the innocent.

The gathering meets at Caiaphas's villa, and the narrator mentions that Peter followed as far as the courtyard (v. 57–58). This is a non sequitur, of course, since we have just been told (v. 56) that he and the rest of the Twelve (except Judas) fled at Jesus's arrest. The narrator wants us to have an inside view of the proceedings, so puts Peter on the scene as a putative source of information. Initial attempts to find incriminating witnesses fail; then finally two accuse Jesus of claiming he could destroy the temple and rebuild it in three days (vv. 59–61). This appears to be a distortion of what Jesus said (23:37–39; 24:2), but the mere prediction of the temple's destruction sufficed to incite opponents to seek the death penalty for the prophet Jeremiah.[3]

The high priest challenges Jesus to respond to the accusation, but he remains silent (vv. 62–63a; compare Isa 53:7). Caiaphas then orders Jesus to declare whether or not he is the Messiah (v. 63b). Unlike Mark 14:62, where the narrative has Jesus affirm that identity, the Matthean version asserts that "you [singular] have said so" (v. 64a). The text continues with a prophecy of the parousia of the Human One, using imagery from Dan 7:13, and depicts Caiaphas as charging Jesus with blasphemy (vv. 64b–65), which is a capital offense (Lev 24:10–16). The rest of the Sanhedrin agree with Caiaphas and

3. It is not clear why prediction of the temple's destruction should be viewed as a capital offense, but see Jer 7:1–15; 26:1–8.

The narrative mentions two witnesses make this accusation against Jesus. Their mutual corroboration is what makes their testimony actionable. The Torah (Deut 19:15) requires at least two eyewitnesses for a conviction, especially for a capital crime.

affirm that Jesus deserves death (v. 66). The narrator portrays the council members as physically abusing Jesus and jeering at him (vv. 67–68)—a detail drawn from GMark but not historically plausible.

There actually is nothing blasphemous in what Jesus says, since he does not use the name of God nor identify himself as the coming Human One. The Matthean community certainly identifies Jesus as the Messiah and prophesied Human One, but to them, such identifications would be blasphemous only if they were false. The scene thus highlights what is at stake between the followers of Jesus and the Jewish authorities: the Matthean community's foundational claims about Jesus's identity are viewed as sacrilegious by the non-Christ-believing Jews. Either Jesus is God's eschatological emissary or he is a deceptive liar deserving of death. The gospel presents no opportunity for compromise.

Peter's Denial (26:69–75)

The vignette with Peter is presented as if it takes place while the Sanhedrin is considering potential evidence against Jesus. A slave woman notices Peter loitering in the courtyard and comments, "You also were with Jesus the Galilean," but Peter denies it (vv. 69–70). Peter withdraws toward the gate of the house, yet he does not retreat far enough. Another slave girl sees him and tells the others nearby that "this man was with Jesus the Nazorean," but Peter more vehemently denies it (vv. 71–72). Yet a third time Peter is charged as being one of Jesus's disciples; a cock crows in the midst of Peter's yet more vociferous and irreligious denial (vv. 73–74). Hearing the rooster, Peter leaves Caiaphas's house and begins to sob bitterly, remembering Jesus's prediction of this threefold denial (v. 75). This image of Peter going into the unprotected street to weep and wail—the outer darkness—also reminds the audience of the earlier threat (Matt 10:33) of what will happen to those who deny Jesus.

Jesus Is Remanded to Pilate (27:1–2)

The narrator briefly returns to the Sanhedrin. The text is a bit confused, since the prior scene with the Sanhedrin culminated in the group deciding that Jesus should die, and morning already was beginning to break (as indicated by the cock crowing in the scene with Peter). The narrator repeats both details here (27:1) and adds that the council had Jesus bound and handed him over to Pilate (v. 2). Roman justice will be viewed in the light of day.

Judas's Repentance and Suicide (27:3–10)

The Matthean scribes add a scene depicting Judas repenting of his betrayal and affirming Jesus's innocence (vv. 3–4). Because his name is cognate to Judah, perhaps they mean to portray him as representative of unbelieving Israel, a lost disciple modeling a "lost tribe." For whatever reason, the scribal evangelists portray Judas as filled with remorse, admitting his sin in collaborating with the religious leaders and attempting to return the bribe they had given him. The priests and elders reject Judas; they care nothing for his repentance: "What's it to us? That's your lookout" (27:4b AT). Poor Judas not only cut himself off from Jesus and the other disciples; now he is scorned by the collaborators on the other side as well.

Judas throws the money into the temple (see also Zech 11:12–13)—figuratively putting the blame for Jesus's death on the temple authorities and perhaps on God as well—and then goes off and hangs himself (v. 5).[4] In this version of the suicide, the priests collect the coins and use them to buy a plot of land to create a cemetery for gentiles, calling it "Field of Blood" (vv. 6–8). The Matthean scribes engage in a creative conflation of various elements of the prophetic tradition (Zech 11:12–13; Jer 19:10–11; 32:6–9) to assert that this purchase fulfills what Jeremiah had prophesied (vv. 9–10). Although the scribes present some of this text as a direct quote from the prophet, they are mistaken on that detail.

The Trial Before Pilate (27:11–14)

The scene now shifts to an unspecified location in the presence of Pontius Pilate, the Roman prefect. Pilate does not ask Jesus about anything directly related to the hearing before the Sanhedrin. (The audience probably is expected to infer that the Jewish leaders informed Pilate of the results of those proceedings when they handed Jesus over to him.) Roman law does not regulate what Jews might consider blasphemy, thus the Sanhedrin's stated reason for viewing Jesus as worthy of death would have no salience

4. Another version of Judas's suicide appears in Acts 1:18–19. The two versions do not agree in any details other than the purchase of a field with the bribe money and the property name, the Field of Blood. In the Acts version, Judas himself uses the funds to buy the field.

for Pilate. Neither would the messianic title make any sense to a Roman official. But the Matthean scribes depict non-Jews using the title "King of the Jews" for Jesus (e.g., 2:2; 27:29, 37), and they equate that moniker with the Jewish title "Messiah." So, while the Sanhedrin asked Jesus whether he was the Messiah, here we see Pilate confronting Jesus about whether he is King (*Basileius*) of the Jews.

Jesus responds to Pilate's question the same way he replied when Caiaphas asked whether he is the Messiah: "You [singular] say so" (27:11). Although not mentioned before, apparently the priests and elders are also in attendance; we hear that they make further accusations—of precisely what nature remains unstated—but Jesus offers no reply (v. 12). Pilate questions why Jesus makes no effort to defend himself and is amazed when Jesus remains unmoved by Pilate's urging (vv. 13–14).

An Amnesty and a Death Sentence (27:15–26)

The narrative claims that Pilate had a "custom" of releasing one prisoner each year at Passover and that he left up to the crowd the specific choice of which prisoner would be reprieved (v. 15). GMatthew gets this tradition from Mark 15:6, and it seems the Matthean scribes did not check its validity. There is no historical evidence to support this assertion; in fact, all the historical evidence concerning Pilate's behavior while prefect of Judea militates against such a claim. GLuke omits this scene, which implies that the evangelist's extensive research (Luke 1:1–4) agreed with contemporary historians in falsifying this alleged custom. The scene should be read figuratively, showing two opposing models of messiahship, rather than as a report of historical events.

The scene presents two men named Jesus, each viewed as "son of the father" (*bar-Abbas*) and each under arrest for a serious crime. The Matthean scribes exclude the Markan detail that Jesus Barabbas was among "the insurrectionists who had committed murder during the insurrection" (Mark 15:7), but they do name Barabbas a "notable" prisoner (27:16). Pilate is depicted as presenting a choice to the crowd: "Whom do you want me to release for you, Jesus Barabbas or Jesus who is called the Messiah?" (v. 17). The omniscient narrator avers that Pilate posed the choice because "he realized that it was out of envy that they had handed [Jesus of Nazareth] over" (v. 18). This imputation of motives to "them" (presumably the elders of Jerusalem) has no support in the earlier narrative—for example, in the scene of the hearing before the Sanhedrin—and reveals the scribal evangelists' efforts to deflect responsibility away from Pilate and the Roman regime and onto the Jewish authorities.

A unique vignette added by the Matthean scribes highlights this move to exonerate the Romans, including Pilate himself, and places the responsibility for Jesus's execution on the Jewish leaders and the mob they controlled. The narrator tells us that, while he was awaiting the crowd's response to the question of which prisoner to reprieve, Pilate received a message from his wife telling him to "have nothing to do with that innocent man, for today I have suffered a great deal because of a dream about him" (v. 19). As we have seen, dreams are used as key modes of divine revelation in this gospel (1:20; 2:12, 13, 19, 22), both for Jews (Joseph) and gentiles (the Magi). The audience certainly would be attentive to such a warning, conveyed to this high-class Roman woman, and the narrator provides no response from Pilate to subvert the impact of his wife's message.

Meanwhile, Jesus's opponents among "the chief priests and elders" are portrayed as inciting the crowd to ask that Jesus Barabbas be released rather than Jesus of Nazareth. As mentioned earlier, the historicity of this passage is in serious doubt. The Matthean scribes use this exchange to highlight their contention that "the crowd," under the influence of the Jewish leaders in Jerusalem, would rather have a false messiah, Jesus Barabbas, than the true one, Jesus of Nazareth.[5] The crowd is cast in the position of a jury when Pilate is said to ask them, "Then what should I do with Jesus who is called the Messiah?" and they reply, "Let him be crucified!" (v. 22) This places the onus for Jesus's execution squarely on the shoulders of the crowd rather than on the Roman prefect—a point reinforced by the Matthean Pilate's protest of Jesus's innocence (v. 23), the handwashing motif (v. 24), and the crowd's asseveration that they accept responsibility: "His blood be upon us and upon our children" (v. 25). The story says Pilate conceded to the crowd, releasing Barabbas and handing Jesus over to be scourged and crucified (v. 26).

Routine punishment for a noncitizen when convicted of a crime in a Roman court began with flogging, that is, being beaten with a barbed whip

5. A verbal double entendre appears here in the Greek text. Pilate is said to ask which of the two prisoners the crowd wants him to *apolysō* to/for them. Typically translated "release" in this verse, *apolysō* also can mean "let die." Thus, the Matthean scribes have Pilate offer the release of Jesus of Nazareth or the chance to let him die for the people. The crowd's later affirmation that they take Jesus's blood upon themselves and their descendants picks up on this imagery of covenant sacrifice (26:28).

that tore off strips of skin and cut into the underlying muscle. Whatever other penalty was deemed to fit the specific crime, the scourged person, now bleeding from multiple wounds, would be left scarred for life and perhaps maimed as well. Since Jesus has been condemned to death, the scourging would likely have included his arms and legs as well as back. Because of the loss of blood and severe trauma to the person's system, flogging was viewed as a way to hasten the dying process for crucifixion victims—a rather perverse type of mercy indeed!

Note that the Matthean scribes do not describe Jesus being scourged; they simply state that Pilate had it done. To provide a description certainly would undercut the narrative spin that makes the Roman prefect reluctant to have Jesus executed, in effect declaring him innocent and putting the onus of the decision on the Jewish authorities and the mob they had mobilized. Historically speaking, Jesus would have been scourged by Roman soldiers before his execution.

It is imperative to remember that the portrayal of the trial before Pilate is a work of creative history drawn from a prophetic interpretation of the Jewish Bible. The scene with Pilate would not have been believed by any of Jesus's contemporaries, who knew Pilate was a brutal and vindictive autocrat. Even among Romans, Pilate was viewed as harsh, his measures unreasonably severe. By 36 CE, there had been so many serious complaints about the prefect's behavior that Vitellius, the legate to Syria, had Pilate recalled to Rome to stand trial for his conduct in the province of Judea. Pilate was charged with cruelty and oppression, including executing people without a proper trial—a detail that makes the gospel's trial scene particularly suspect.

In other words, this is a theological narrative, not history. The characters of Jesus, Pilate, and the Jewish leaders play stereotypical roles drawn from the Bible: the prophet, the recalcitrant king or other government official(s), and the Israelite people. The Matthean scribes tell their predominantly Jewish audience: Like our ancestors who spurned the earlier prophets, the Jewish leaders of Jesus's day were not willing to accept him as an authentic emissary from God, much less to recognize his true status as the divinely sent Messiah. The warning from Claudia Procula to her husband, Pilate, is intended for the entire audience of the gospel: "[Let there be] nothing between you and this righteous person" (v. 19 AT), that is, let nothing separate you from Jesus, whose blood indeed is "upon us and upon our children."

Jesus's Execution and Burial

Scourging and Mockery (27:27–31)

The narrator remarks on a change of venue now that Jesus has been sentenced. Pilate's soldiers take him to the praetorium, that is, the residence of the praetor. Pilate's seat of government was Caesarea Maritima on the Mediterranean coast, but he came to Jerusalem for the great pilgrimage festivals—not out of devotion but to prevent anti-Roman riots and be on the spot to suppress the crowds if they became unruly. It is not clear whether the praetorium mentioned in the gospel narrative was Herod's old palace in the west of Jerusalem or the Antonia fortress northwest of the temple area. For purposes of the story, the category of the location is more important than the geography. The Roman prefect condemned Jesus; Roman soldiers arrested Jesus and took him to Roman property in Jerusalem to scourge him; Roman soldiers followed Pilate's orders to crucify him.

Instead of depicting the scourging, the Matthean scribes (following Mark 15:16–20) present a scene in which Roman soldiers gather their "whole cohort" of six hundred soldiers to mock Jesus and cane him (vv. 27, 30). The narrator says they stripped Jesus (i.e., removing his *himation* and tunic), draped a red legionary's cloak around him (Mark 15:17), crowned him with a garland of thorns, put a reedy mock scepter in his right hand, and knelt before Jesus, hailing him as "King of the Jews" (vv. 28–29). The soldiers are said to have spat on Jesus and caned him (v. 30), which is the closest the narrator gets to anything like flogging. The scene concludes with the totally unrealistic detail of the soldiers putting Jesus's own clothes back on him before taking him out to be crucified; the Matthean scribes want to set up the later scene in which the Golgotha guards cast lots for his garments (v. 35).

The Crucifixion of Jesus (27:32–44)

The narrator begins the crucifixion scene with what seems like an aside, the mention of a North African, Simon, from Cyrenaica, whom the Roman soldiers pressed into carrying the cross of Jesus (v. 32). As mentioned earlier (see the discussion of 5:41), Roman soldiers garrisoned in the provinces were authorized to requisition goods and services of the "natives." Typically, convicts were required to carry their own implements of destruction—in a case like this, the crossbeam, since the vertical beam was permanently installed at the place of crucifixion—so the rationale for stating that Simon was chosen to carry the cross for Jesus is not clear, although all three Synoptic Gospels include the vignette. Like the suppression of the flogging scene, putting Jesus's crossbeam literally on Simon's shoulders may reflect an attempt by the evangelists to minimize the graphic description of Jesus's suffering, especially since virtually every member of the original audience would have witnessed a crucifixion at some point. Mark 15:21 includes personal details about this Simon, which suggests he was well known to the Markan community. The Matthean scribes omit those family connections; perhaps their community did not know Simon personally so were not expected to recognize the names of his relatives. GJohn takes this editorial move one step further and simply omits Simon altogether (see John 19:17).

Upon arriving at Golgotha (about one-third mile from the praetorium, if the Antonia fortress location is correct), the soldiers prepare Jesus for crucifixion. They give him a drink of the sour wine that was part of their typical ration, but he took one taste and refused any more (vv. 33–34; compare Ps 69:22). Prisoners were crucified "naked," which means without a tunic, cloak, or any other outer garment; if the person wore a loincloth or breechclout under the tunic, that probably was left alone.[6] The act of disrobing Jesus again is not mentioned—another clue that he actually was not redressed after having been stripped for flogging—but a subtle "prophecy-fulfillment" detail is added when the soldiers cast lots for the garments (v. 35b; compare Ps 22:19). Nor is the act of crucifixion detailed, so we do not know precisely how Jesus was attached to the cross, whether by nails or rope ties or a combination thereof. For a community whose members are all too familiar with this form of the death penalty, lack of such details allows them to envision Jesus in any of the other individuals they have seen executed and perhaps also prevents the severe kinds of post-traumatic stress reactions for any whose intimate family or friends have been victims of such an agonizing death.

The narrative goes on to mention a *titulus* that was hung on the cross to specify what crime led to this execution: "This is Jesus, the King [*Basileus*] of the Jews" (v. 37). In other words, Jesus was convicted of subversion, opposing the *basileia* of God to that of Rome. In this respect, the Romans were correct. Jesus preached a divine *basileia* opposed to every kind of human empire,

6. Track-and-field athletic contests in the Greco-Roman world involved participation "naked," but the word in that context meant wearing nothing but a loincloth. Apparently, such an undergarment did not count as being clothed.

every social or political structure that fosters power over others rather than servanthood and acceptance of God as the sole *Basileius*. As befitting his crime, Jesus is said to have been crucified between two *lestai* (revolutionaries or brigands [v. 38]). There might well have been more than three execution victims that day, but the narrative highlights these figures to emphasize that the Roman authorities viewed Jesus as a revolutionary.

The narrator mentions passersby taunting Jesus: "Save yourself" (vv. 39–40). Artistic renditions of the scene often make Golgotha look like a place apart, but that is only because it was outside the Holy City. Roman crucifixions routinely took place along the major highways leading from one town to another. In the case of Jesus and the others crucified with him, hundreds of pilgrims coming toward or leaving Jerusalem would have seen these executions.[7]

Conflating all of Jesus's Jewish opponents into one group, the Matthean scribes say that "the chief priests with the scribes and elders" also mocked him, deriding his claims to be the King of Israel and Son of God (vv. 41–43). They aver that they "will believe in him" if Jesus proves his power by coming down from the cross (v. 42b). The text has them quoting Ps 22:9 as part of their jeering, which shows the stylized way the Matthean scribes have presented these taunts.[8] Even the two *lestai* harass Jesus in these terms (v. 44), which implies they were Jewish revolutionaries like Barabbas is portrayed elsewhere (e.g., Mark 15:7).

Jesus Dies on the Cross (27:45–56)

The Matthean scribes reveal the death throes of creation while Jesus endures his torturous death on the cross. When it should shine the brightest, the sun is darkened from noon until the ninth hour (three p.m. [v. 45]). Midafternoon arrives to hear Jesus crying out in the words of the biblical lament, "My God, my God, why have you forsaken me?" (Ps 22:2; v. 46).[9] Some onlookers mistake Jesus's cry and think he is invoking Elijah (vv. 47–49). Jesus

7. In fact, the Roman writer Quintilian (ca. 35–96 CE) avers that the major highways are used for such executions to ensure that as many people as possible see and are struck with fear. See Quintilian, *Lesser Declamations*, 274.

8. Compare to Wis 2:12–20, which seems to provide the framework for this portrayal of the hecklers.

9. The Matthean scribes retain the Aramaic quotation from Mark 15:34, although they modify the vocative to the Hebrew *Eli* (rather than the original *Eloi*), perhaps to make the onlookers' confusion about Elijah more intelligible.

utters yet another wordless cry and "sends up" his spirit, handing it back to God (v. 50). More portents now appear and many things are sundered: the temple veil is rent in twain, rocks are split, earthquakes cause tombs to open, and the bodies of "many holy ones" were raised from death, prefiguring the resurrection of Jesus himself and said to be confirmed by many witnesses (vv. 51–53). This series of closed items metaphorically being opened marks the unveiling of the fullness of divine revelation. The veil before the holy of holies in the temple, which marked as out of bounds that space of ultimate proximity to God, no longer operates; through the life and death of Jesus, God has been made immanent to every human person. Similarly, the earthquakes and uprisings of the just show the dramatic transition that precedes the culmination of the divine plan, with resurrection of the just as proof that the final age is coming upon the earth.

The Roman soldiers guarding the crucified prisoners are said to respond to these portents with the fearful affirmation "truly this was a son of a god" (v. 54 AT). Christian translations of the verse change the text into "this was the Son of God," but that puts into the gentile soldier's mouth a monotheism that Romans did not understand and indeed saw as ridiculous. Unlike Latin, the Greek language does have a definite article ("the"), but none appear in this phrase. Since English also has an indefinite article ("a," "an"), foreign nouns used without a definite article are legitimately translated without an article (e.g., "son of god") or with the indefinite article ("a son of a god"); but it is erroneous to insert the definite article where there is none. For a Roman to speak of "a son of god" was not an affirmation of the faith of Nicaea, which is what the definite article implies.

The Roman soldiers are depicted as using language that would be applied to Hercules and other demigods of their culture and most recently had been applied to Caesar Augustus and every emperor since then. The phrase thus may have a dangerous political salience, but its colloquial meaning is more like "this was a really heroic man." Roman soldiers were enculturated into a reverence for an honorable death, one faced with courage, restraint, and emotional equanimity. The well-known line from Horace's *Odes* shaped their military culture: "Dulce et decorum est pro patria mori."[10] Death by crucifixion was about as dishonorable as one could get, but the Matthean scribes knew that Jesus did indeed die for the sake of the nation. The remarks they impute to the Roman soldiers affirm

10. "Sweet and fitting it is to die for the homeland" (*Ode* 3.2.13, in Horace [65–8 BCE], *Carminum liber tertius*).

that Jesus was a heroic figure worthy of honor, in spite of his ignominious mode of execution.

The narrative mentions that "many" women disciples who had traveled with Jesus all the way from Galilee were keeping vigil "at a distance" while Jesus gradually asphyxiated on the cross (v. 55; compare Ps 38:12.) Many have assumed that the women disciples remained when the men fled because women were not at risk of arrest and execution if found in complicity with Jesus, but this is sheer romantic fantasy. Women were not exempt from crucifixion; the key difference between their treatment and that of men is that they were gang-raped by the arresting soldiers before being mounted on the cross.

Unusually for GMatthew, the narrative goes on to list several women by name: "Among them were Mary Magdalene and Mary the mother of James and Joseph, and the mother of the sons of Zebedee" (v. 56). Matthew 13:55 identifies James and Joseph as Jesus's brothers, so this second Mary would be Jesus's mother. The sons of Zebedee are James and John; later Christian tradition identifies their mother as Salome (which agrees with her mention in Mark 16:1). It is curious that the identifications of the last two women follow the cultural norm of situating them with respect to their relationships to men, whereas the Magdalene is named in her own right, identified by the title Jesus had given her. This detail supports her significance for the early Christ believers, including the Matthean community.

Jesus Is Buried (27:57–61)

The narrator sets the burial scene in darkness. The light went out of the world as Jesus was dying (v. 45), which the narrator places soon after three p.m. Now evening has come and Jesus's body still hangs on the cross. Customarily, crucifixion victims remained unburied, their bodies left to rot and be eaten by ravens, dogs, and other scavengers. The Romans viewed the lack of proper burial as a curse, ensuring the person would be consigned to ceaseless wandering in the afterlife. Jews viewed contact with a corpse as conveying ritual impurity (e.g., Num 31:19); it would be very difficult even to walk on the roadway past a crucifixion victim without becoming polluted. Perhaps the Matthean scribes include this scene to reassure the audience that Jesus's body did not become a means of ritual pollution for the nation.

A new disciple, Joseph of Arimathea, is introduced at this late point in the narrative. GMatthew omits the Markan tradition identifying him as a member of the Sanhedrin, simply characterizing Joseph as a wealthy man (v. 57; Mark 15:43). Arimathea (which means "high places") is unknown outside the Bible, but it traditionally is identified with Ramathaim-Zophim, which lies about five miles north of Jerusalem. Joseph is characterized as having direct access to Pilate, and—wonder of wonders—Pilate immediately grants what he asks (v. 58). Joseph is said to receive Jesus's body from the Roman soldiers who were tasked to remove it from the cross. Joseph wraps the body in a clean linen shroud and lays it in a new tomb, rolling a stone across the entrance to seal it, and then returns home (vv. 59–60). Two of Jesus's disciples are there to observe this pious behavior: Mary Magdalene and "the other Mary" (presumably Jesus's mother) remained on the spot, facing the tomb (v. 61). This final detail sets up the women's return on the first day of the week; otherwise, they would not have known where Jesus was buried.

Guards at the Tomb (27:62–66)

The Matthean scribes add a unique scene designed to confute early rumors alleging that some of Jesus's disciples stole his body and lied about him being raised up (28:11–15). The timeline is confused; the narrator mentions that the incident takes place "the next day, the one following the day of preparation [for the Sabbath]," but that would make it the Sabbath day itself, when work is forbidden. The protagonists now are "the chief priests and the Pharisees" (rather than "the chief priests and elders," who figured throughout the arrest and trial). This embassy comes to Pilate to request guards at Jesus's tomb, repeating Jesus's prediction that, "after three days, I will be raised up" (v. 63). Pilate grants the guards, and the vignette ends with the confirmation that the emissaries "went and secured the tomb by fixing a seal to the stone and setting the guard" (vv. 64–65). The detail of setting a seal on the tomb is not part of the request to Pilate but is intended to reassure the audience that there was no chance of tampering with the burial.[11]

11. It also may be intended to hint at Cant 8:6. Compare to Gos. Pet. 28–33, esp. v. 33, which speaks of seven seals, the number appropriate for a last will and testament.

The Resurrection and Great Commission

GMatthew culminates with the stories of the empty tomb, post-resurrection appearances of Jesus, and the Great Commission in which Jesus sends the believers to take the gospel message to "the whole world." While the empty tomb scene is modeled after Mark 16:1–8a, the remainder of this material is unique to GMatthew.

Jesus Is Raised from the Tomb (28:1–10)

As it begins to grow light on the first day of the week, we find two of the women disciples (Mary Magdalene and "the other Mary") returning to the tomb. No reason is given for their return. They carry nothing with them; they have no plans to anoint a body already treated properly for burial by Joseph of Arimathea. They simply return to the last place they saw Jesus. Disciples follow their teacher, so these women disciples show their faithfulness by following even to the tomb. Whereas Peter and the sons of Zebedee claimed they would follow Jesus even unto death, none of the Twelve did so. Only the faithful women disciples live up to this call.

As the two women approach the tomb, a heavenly messenger, clothed in white garments and shining like lightning, descends from heaven amid a great earthquake (27:51–53), rolls the stone up the inclined track to open the tomb, and sits on the rock as if enthroned (28:1–3). The Roman guards, frightened out of their wits, fall down as if struck dead (v. 4). The empty tomb by itself does not prove that Jesus has been raised, so the Matthean scribes have modified the Markan story to depict the women actually seeing the tomb opened. Curiously, the narrator does not mention the breaking of the seal at that point, but the audience would assume that this happened. They are not likely to have imagined the tomb had been previously opened and then closed again before now.

The narrative continues with the angelic messenger "replying" to the women disciples' implied question, reassuring them: "Do not be afraid, for I know that you are looking for Jesus who was crucified. He is not here, for he has been raised, as he said [16:21; 17:23; 20:19]. Come, see the place where he lay" (28:5–6). The messenger then commissions these two women disciples to tell the others that Jesus "has been raised from the dead, and indeed he is going ahead of you to Galilee; there you will see him" (v. 7). The messenger's final remark—"Behold, I have told you"

(v. 7d NABRE)—functions as a formulaic assurance that the entire divine message has been delivered.

The Matthean scribes present the women as being fearful yet overjoyed, and they faithfully run to share the message with the other disciples (v. 8). This "corrects" the Markan story (Mark 16:8a) to fit both what the Matthean community wants to hear of the women and also what they know happened with the gospel of the resurrection. The women were faithful; they did tell the story and made it possible for all of Jesus's disciples to know this story they love to tell.

On the way to take their divinely appointed message to the other disciples, Jesus himself appears to the faithful women. They fall at his feet in worship (compare John 20:17), and Jesus repeats the angelic message, reaffirming that he will appear to the others in Galilee (vv. 9–10). This geographical move provides closure to the gospel, inviting the audience to return to the point where the ministry of Jesus began and build on that foundation. It also may hint at the Galilean location for the Matthean community.

The Guards' Report (28:11–15)

Although the guards seem to have been struck dead at the angelic appearance, at least some of them have recovered enough to report to their superiors. Interestingly, their line of report is to "the chief priests" rather than to Pilate (v. 11). This has led some commentators to infer that the tomb watch was composed of temple guards rather than Roman soldiers, but that is a fallacious conclusion. This scene has been constructed by the Matthean scribes to combat the allegation that the disciples stole Jesus's body from the tomb and then spread the false rumor that he had been raised up by God. The detail with the guards going directly to the temple officials is merely an editorial glitch that hastens the action of the story.

The priests are said to gather the elders to discuss damage-control measures. The narrative clearly assumes that these Jewish leaders believe that Jesus really was raised by God, in accordance with the angelic message and the guards' eyewitness testimony. So, they act not out of disbelief but out of self-interest, attempting to suppress what they know to be the truth. They decide on a strategy of bribery and dissimulation, paying the guards "a large sum of money" to spread the lie that Jesus's disciples came in the night and stole the body while the guards were asleep (vv. 12–13).

Given that the guards would be incriminating themselves for falling asleep while on watch—a capital offense—such a lie would be plausible. The conspirators promise the soldiers to cover their backs so they will not be executed if their story comes to the ears of the *hegemon*, usually translated "governor" but, in this case, better construed as referring to their superior officer, whoever that might be (v. 14). The narrator concludes that the ploy worked: the soldiers "took the money and did as they were directed. And this story is still told among the Judeans to this day" (v. 15).

This vignette demonstrates that, from the perspective of the Matthean community, the dispute between them and non-Christ-believing Jews about the empty tomb concerned not *whether* the tomb was empty but *why*. While this story of a conspiracy to hide the truth of the resurrection puts the Jewish priests and elders in an unenviable position, at least indirectly it also goes some way to excuse those Jews who do not accept the gospel. They are not necessarily hard-hearted; they might simply have been duped by the false shepherds among their leaders.

The Great Commission (28:16–20)

The final scene of GMatthew is called the Great Commission because of the broad scope of the risen Jesus's instructions to the disciples.[12] The location is a mountaintop in Galilee, a detail that goes beyond the message delivered by both the angelic messenger and the risen Jesus but suitable to the new Moses imagery that has been threaded throughout GMatthew. The narrator specifies that the Eleven are present with Jesus (v. 16); this does not exclude other disciples, but the spotlight is on these few men who need to be rehabilitated after abandoning Jesus at his arrest.

When the Eleven see Jesus, they prostrate themselves in worship; yet, the omniscient narrator tells us, they still wavered, doubtful (v. 17). The women disciples in the empty tomb scene come across better; they were afraid, yet joyful, with no shadow of doubt. Perhaps as a measure of reassurance, Jesus affirms that "all authority in heaven and on the earth has been given to me" (v. 18; compare Dan 7:13–14). He then commissions the Eleven as his emissaries: "Go, therefore, make disciples of all nations, baptizing them . . . [and] teaching them to observe all that I have commanded you"

12. It also sometimes is called a "proleptic parousia," perhaps because of the mountaintop setting and the reverence of the Eleven. Jesus's authoritative presence on the mountain provides a foretaste of the final glorious coming of the Human One (26:64), who rightly receives worship.

(vv. 19–20a). Nor will the emissaries be left unaided: "And behold, I am with you always, until the consummation of the age" (v. 20b).

Since only eleven male disciples of Jesus are here named, this scene has been twisted to justify the erasure of the history of women disciples of Jesus—and, later, exclusion of women from ecclesial ministries. On the contrary, the Matthean community knows that Jesus had women disciples (e.g., the women at the crucifixion, burial, and empty tomb scenes), and the Matthean scribes honor the tradition that Jesus appeared first to these women disciples before the Eleven knew Jesus had been raised. In addition, the authors know that the women did not desert Jesus at his arrest; they remained faithful to the end, unlike the Twelve who swore they would undergo death with Jesus but fled when the time came to fulfill that promise.

In fact, the Matthean community knows that the Eleven would never have heard of the resurrection of Jesus if the women disciples had not faithfully carried to them the divine message. So, this commissioning scene is not intended to exclude women disciples nor to imply that only eleven missionaries ever took the gospel of Jesus abroad. It may, however, reflect an insider/outsider division of labor for such evangelistic work. The women take the message to "the brothers," other members of the house of Israel, while the Eleven are sent to "all nations" (v. 19). The Matthean scribes may be recognizing a "separation of spheres" for evangelistic work that recognizes the preeminence of women evangelists among the Jewish community while men evangelists take the lead in the "public" sphere of non-Jews, who may be culturally less inclined to listen to women's testimony. Such a dismissal of women's testimony appears explicitly in Luke 24:9–11, where the Eleven themselves are said to disbelieve the message. Anticipating that the women might have less credibility with non-Jews, the Matthean scribes present the female evangelists working among "insiders" who know and respect them while male disciples take the gospel to "outsiders."

It also is important to note the content of that evangelistic message: making disciples means "baptizing them . . . and teaching them to obey everything that I have commanded you" (28:19–20a). Conversion is not a head trip. Disciples are baptized into the name, but that is only the beginning. True conversion involves observing the divine commandments, especially those Jesus has emphasized, and following his interpretation of them. Matthean discipleship involves the *works* of faith, not mere verbal or intellectual assent. Disciples imitate the life of Jesus, follow his precepts, and recognize that everyone will be judged on that basis, not on lip service.

Conclusions

This final section of GMatthew, the passion-resurrection narrative, conveys five key ideas that have been put before the audience at various points throughout the entire gospel but now are brought to a climax. First, Jesus was the true Messiah sent to inaugurate God's *basileia*, which is already starting to take hold among Jesus's disciples and will be revealed fully at the glorious parousia of the Human One at the end of the age. Second, that *basileia* will overthrow all human power structures, so those in current positions of power (like the priests and elders in Jerusalem) instinctively oppose it. Third, thinking they can prevent the coming of God's *basileia* by killing God's messenger, the Jerusalem leaders collaborate in the Roman execution of Jesus. Fourth, God's will cannot be thwarted nor the divine message quashed: God vindicates Jesus's innocence of any alleged crimes and validates the truth of Jesus's gospel of the *basileia* by raising him up to fullness of life "on the third day," the "day of the Lord" and time of restoration of the entire people of Israel (Hos 6:2). Finally, Jesus has commissioned his women and men disciples to share this gospel of the *basileia* to those both within Israel and among all the gentile nations, baptizing them as a mark of entrance into the community of believers and teaching them to follow the way of Jesus, living out all of his commandments; thereby, Jesus himself will be present with them "until the consummation of the age" (28:20 AT), that is, until his glorious parousia as the Human One.

Review and Discussion Questions

A. Review Questions

1. Why would the Jewish leaders have been concerned about having Jesus arrested during the Passover Festival?
2. How many legal hearings or trials does GMatthew show Jesus undergoing before he is condemned to death?
3. Who finally was responsible for Jesus's execution? At this period in Judean history, who had the legal authority to pass sentence in a capital crime and execute the convicted party?

B. Discussion Questions

1. What does the anointing scene (Matt 26:6–13) tell us about the role of prophetic women in the early Jesus movement?

2. GMatthew shows both Judas and Peter betraying Jesus—Judas, by collaborating with Jesus's opponents; Simon Peter, by disowning his association with Jesus. GMatthew tells us that Judas repented (Matt 27:3–10), and did so early enough that he easily could have been arrested and executed with Jesus. All that is said of Simon Peter is that he wept to realize Jesus's prediction was correct (26:69–75), but he never put himself at risk by going to the authorities and correcting his false statement. In spite of these facts, the interpretive tradition has made Judas out to be the only betrayer and has turned Peter into a saint. Why do you think this is the case? Do you think it is fair? How so or how not?
3. What function is served by the amnesty scene with Jesus bar Abbas? What theological message does it convey?
4. Unlike the noncanonical Gospel of Peter, none of the canonical gospels depicts any of the disciples actually seeing the resurrection of Jesus. Instead, the affirmation that God had raised Jesus up from among the dead was divinely revealed to the women disciples who discovered the empty tomb. GMatthew admits that these faithful women were the sole messengers of the resurrection, the first apostles in the technical sense of the term, but the women disciples seem to fade from view as soon as they pass this message along to the "brothers." Do you think the scribal evangelists tried to downplay the women's importance (e.g., by not including them in the Great Commission)? How so or how not? What significance, if any, do you see in this gender dynamic?

Chapter 10
GMATTHEW IN EMERGING CHRISTIAN DISCOURSE

The Reception of GMatthew in the Early Church

GMatthew seems to have become a dominant gospel early in the first few centuries CE. Writing intentionally to replace and expand upon GMark, which included insufficient guidance for the Matthean community of the 80s in the aftermath of the failed Jewish revolt, the scribal evangelists expanded the first gospel by over seven thousand words, creating a version 162 percent as long as GMark. In the process, they absorbed over 600 of the 661 verses of GMark (nearly 91 percent) and reworked details of the storyline to include an infancy narrative, five "books of Jesus" (like the five "books of Moses" in the Torah), and a passion-resurrection narrative that includes post-resurrection appearances with Jesus commissioning both women and men evangelists to carry the gospel of the *basileia* and make disciples of Israel and all the nations.

Expansions like the Sermon on the Mount, the last judgment scene, and unique Matthean parables—which are easily read as allegories so are less confusing than many of the Markan parables—make GMatthew easily accessible for catechesis. The teaching of a particular prayer, presented as coming from Jesus himself, had tremendous appeal for early communities of believers who sought the best way to address the God of the universe, whom Jesus addressed as Abba. The Matthean Jesus gives the community authority to develop its own structures, "the keys to the kingdom," and includes processes for resolving internal differences that help the community retain that autonomy vis-à-vis the wider Greco-Roman world. If one was looking for a gospel that would serve a developing church in a period when the war had ceased to be a lively part of the congregation's imagination, GMatthew would win hands down over GMark.

Two examples of later early Christian texts, the Didache and the collection of letters of Ignatius of Antioch, provide some evidence of the impact of GMatthew in the developing Christian tradition. The Didache probably was completed in Syria about the turn of the first century, so is both geographically and chronologically closer to GMatthew than the works of Ignatius. While Ignatius comes from Antioch, his letters are addressed primarily to recipients in Asia Minor and date to the end of his life (ca. 107 CE). Neither the Didache nor Ignatius mentions GMatthew explicitly, but both have close quotations and allusions to Matthean material, while shaping that material to suit their own circumstances and purposes.

The development of the New Testament canon also highlights the centrality of GMatthew, as can be seen in the discussions of Origen of Alexandria and Eusebius Pamphilus. Overall, we can see the success of the Matthean community in composing a story that would replace the earlier GMark and that Christians throughout the centuries would love to tell.

The Didache

One of the more popular early Christian texts is called the Teaching of the Twelve Apostles, commonly shortened to the Didache (the Teaching).[1] As the title indicates, this anonymous document purports to convey the teaching of Jesus's early apostles. The text comprises four parts that likely were created independently over a period of time before being collected into this church handbook at about the turn of the second century.[2] The first section (chs. 1–6) focuses on a traditional wisdom motif called the "Two Ways" doctrine; it outlines the way of life versus death, righteousness versus injustice. The next section shifts from catechesis to more of a church manual. Chapters 7–10 provide directions on how Christian rituals should

1. The translation of the Didache quoted herein is that of Kirsopp Lake in LCL. Compare to the Riddle translation in *ANF* 7.

2. The traditional assumption of the Didache's dependence upon GMatthew (or pre-Matthean materials) is contested (*inter alii*) by Garrow (*Gospel of Matthew's Dependence*), who promotes a date to 50–70 CE, before GMatthew. This proposal has not been persuasive.

be done, including instructions for baptism, fasting, prayer, and the eucharistic meal. This is followed by a section on ecclesial ministries, including apostles, prophets, bishops, and deacons (chs. 11–15). The collection concludes with a prophecy of the second coming (ch. 16).

The Didache shares material with GMatthew and traditionally has been viewed as dependent upon the gospel, or at least upon some of the pre-Matthean material used by the scribal evangelists when creating the gospel. The "Two Ways" section in Did. 2–6 may precede the completion of GMatthew, since it includes fairly common sets of virtues and vices, some of which derive from commonplace moral lists and others that have strong resonances with Proverbs and Ben Sirach or that quote or closely paraphrase portions of Exodus, Deuteronomy, Colossians, and Ephesians. However, a pre-Matthean date is not likely for Did. 1, which evinces significant areas of overlap with GMatthew.

This first chapter of the Didache seems to draw directly from the Sermon on the Mount in Matt 5–7, including the sayings about the greatest commandment, turning the other cheek, and loving one's enemies. Some of the sayings seem to have been modified in a cautionary vein, so come across more sternly than in GMatthew. For example, the Golden Rule is reported here not as a positive injunction but as a prohibition: "Whatsoever thou wouldst not have done to thyself, do not thou to another" (Did. 1.2b). While almsgiving is supported, the audience is not encouraged to give freely, so that "the left hand does not know what the right hand is doing" (Matt 6:3); rather, the injunction is qualified: "Let thine alms sweat into thine hands until thou knowest to whom thou art giving" (Did. 1.6). Yet, the author reveals ambivalence on this point in Did. 1.5 and 4.5–8, which seem to return to the more generous rule expressed by Jesus. Such modifications are to be expected in a later text; traditions often get more stringent over time. The traditional scholarly view that the Didache builds on GMatthew, rather than vice versa, is supported by this kind of redactional evidence.

Once we progress to the ritual material in Did. 7–10, more overlap with GMatthew appears. The baptismal formula in Did. 7 is virtually identical to that in Matt 28:19, while the prayer instructions in Did. 8.2 repeat the Matthean version of the Lord's Prayer (Matt 6:9–13), although with the addition of the liturgical doxology ("for thine is the power and the glory forever"). The audience is encouraged to "pray thus three times a day" (Did. 8.3), which again expands on the material in GMatthew, where the audience is simply told to pray thus when they pray. While

Matt 6:16–18 describes how to fast, Did. 8.1 does not repeat that material; instead of being warned not to *behave* like the hypocrites (Matt 6:16), the Didache's audience is warned to avoid fasting *on the same days* as the hypocrites. This kind of detail again supports a later date for the Didache, since it assumes a more developed form of organization with the community having designated fast days.

The section on the Eucharist (Did. 9–10) includes an outline of an actual eucharistic prayer, rather than the simple institution narrative found in GMatthew. The prayer includes intercessions for the church, already envisioned as spread to "the ends of the earth" and needing to be gathered thence at the parousia (Did. 9.4; see also 10.5). Some elements of this portion of the Didache appear in liturgical prayers to this day.

The set of prayers includes a thanksgiving after the meal and prayer for the swift coming of the final age. The Aramaic prayer *Marana tha* ("Our Lord! Come!") highlights the continuing anticipation of the parousia and implies that the Didache community agrees with GMatthew that Jesus is the coming Human One.

A liturgical rule excludes non-baptized persons from participating in the eucharistic meal. This kind of detail again suggests a more highly structured ecclesial community and therefore a later date of composition than GMatthew.

The section in Did. 11–15 is sometimes called a "church order" because it makes recommendations for how the community should handle itinerant missionaries, preachers, and prophets, and also provides a list of qualifications for local church leaders. The authors are wary of roving missionaries, and the text hints that the community either has had personal experience with false missionaries or has heard cautionary tales about them. The community should not be gullible or open themselves to charlatans.

First of all, a doctrinal orthodoxy test is recommended (Did. 11.2). If the missionary's teaching is orthodox, then the second test is to see how long they ask to be fed and housed at the expense of the community. The community is encouraged to brand as a false teacher (or false apostle or prophet) any itinerant preacher who stays more than one or two days (11.5), or who asks for money when leaving (11.6), or who prophesies that the community should hold a charitable banquet and then eats of it (11.9), or who teaches false doctrine (11.10). Those who purport to be prophets should be judged by whether their behavior conforms to Christian standards (11.7–8). If a prophet lives up to these standards but does not teach others to do so, that should not concern the community (11.11); only the converse is a problem, since that is the very definition of hypocrisy. Beware the avaricious charlatan but not the one who encourages selfless generosity: "But whosoever shall say in a spirit 'Give me money, or something else,' you shall not listen to him; but if he tell you to give on behalf of others in want, let none judge him" (11.12).

Didache 12 addresses the issue of the average Christian believer who is traveling for one reason or another. They should be welcomed but are to meet the same litmus test of time; they should not impose on the community's hospitality for more than three days. If they want to settle in the community, the community needs a guarantee that they can provide for themselves through their work. Any who refuse to pull their own weight are hypocrites "making traffic of Christ" (12.5); the community should beware of them. Whether this means expulsion is not clear. In comparison with the activities of Jesus and the disciples in GMatthew (who very likely spent more than three days at a time in a given place), this rule shows a warier group than those given an unqualified command to "welcome the stranger" (Matt 25:35).

The Didache community anticipates cases of prophets or teachers who want to settle among them. If those persons have been verified as true prophets or teachers (via the tests in Did. 11), they should be allowed to stay and are worthy of support (Did. 13.1–2). In fact, the community should give to these charismatic leaders the firstfruits "of the produce of the winepress and of the threshing-floor and of oxen and sheep, . . . for they are your high priests" (13.3). Similar sharing is stipulated for the firstfruits of bread, every "jar of wine or oil, . . . of money also and clothes, and of all your possessions" (13.5–7). If the community does not have a prophet, then the firstfruits should be given to the poor (13.4). In comparison to Jesus's injunction that perfection involves "sell[ing] all that you have and giv[ing] to the poor" (Matt 19:21) and the earliest disciples' practice of a common purse, the regulations about firstfruits provide evidence of an established residential community. That does not necessarily entail one later in time, since Jesus also had some residential disciples who did not travel with him (e.g., Mary, Martha, and Lazarus of Bethany), but the diversion of temple tithes to support of local community leaders implies a post-70 CE date, after the Jerusalem temple had been destroyed.

Didache 14 introduces "the Lord's Day," Sunday, as the day of worship (rather than the Sabbath). This nomenclature derives from the resurrection narrative in Matt 28, where the first day of the week becomes the day opening to the fullness of the *basileia*. Based on Mal 1:6–14, the text encourages ritual purity, especially noting the need to confess transgressions and reconcile quarrels before joining the meeting (14.1–2; Matt 5:23–24). The theme of misbehavior and reconciliation recurs in Did 15.3, where the community is encouraged to shun those who have done wrong to a neighbor. This section seems to fit better after the earlier section on the Eucharist (Did. 7–10), so the editors evidently composed this part of the document from earlier sources but without spending too much time arranging those materials thematically.

Didache 15 returns to the discussion of community leaders in chs. 11–13, now attending for the first time to "bishops and deacons," who seem to have responsibility for financial affairs (as seen, e.g., in 1 Tim 3). Interestingly, remarks about reproofs and wrongdoing appear in this section, so the community seems particularly attuned to the possibility of financial malfeasance by such community officers. Perhaps as a corrective, this chapter concludes with an injunction to do the works appropriate to a disciple: "But your prayers and alms and all your acts perform as ye find in the Gospel of our Lord" (15.5; compare to Matt 28:20a on the commission to teach future disciples to observe all of Jesus's commandments). GJohn has a similar focus on Jesus's commandments (e.g., John 14:15, 21), but the Didache's focus is much more likely to come from GMatthew since it shows no evidence of other similarities with GJohn.

The final chapter of the Didache returns to the eschatological theme introduced earlier, in the eucharistic prayer (Did. 9–10), and here highlighted by a series of injunctions to vigilance and warnings about the turmoil and tests that will come at the end of the age. Some of the language sounds similar to that in the Apocalypse of John (e.g., "the deceiver of the world," the fiery trial, and heavenly signs in 16.4–6), yet it also appears in texts like Paul's Thessalonian correspondence (e.g., 1 Thess 4:16; 2 Thess 1:7–10; 2:3–4, 7–12), so the themes likely were well known—and well traveled—in early Christian circles.

While the Didache's mention of the trumpet announcing the parousia of the Lord on the clouds before the last judgment fits well with the description in Matt 24:29–31, the Didache does not agree with the type of eternal punishment for the wicked that appears in Matt 25:46a. Instead, Did. 16.7 insists that only the just will share in the resurrection; the unjust dead simply remain dead. The primary purpose of this eschatological section seems to be identical to that repeatedly noted in GMatthew: be ready. And, as in GMatthew, readiness is a communal affair: "Be frequently gathered together seeking the things which are profitable for your souls, for the whole time of your faith shall not profit you except ye be found perfect at the last time" (Did 16.2).

Ignatius of Antioch

The earliest Christian author to directly quote GMatthew is Ignatius Theophoros (ca. 35–ca. 107 CE), the third bishop of Antioch in Syria, who was condemned to death *ad bestias* under the emperor Trajan (who reigned 98–117).[3] While Ignatius was under arrest and being taken to be martyred in Rome (in the famous Flavian Colosseum), he composed a series of letters to the church in Ephesus and four other churches in its vicinity (Magnesia, Philadelphia, Smyrna, and Tralles), as well as to the church in Rome and to a contemporary Smyrnaean church leader named Polycarp.[4] The letters to the five churches in Asia mention a few doctrinal issues, almost as asides, but they focus on the community's relationship to the bishop; because of that focus, Ignatius's letters often are viewed as the earliest justification for the monarchical episcopate. The letter to the church in Rome, on the other hand, is sent to a community Ignatius anticipates meeting only when he arrives in their city for execution. He tells them of his desire for martyrdom and appeals to them to avoid interfering with the death sentence.

Several details of Ignatius's letters show traces of GMatthew. *Smyrnaeans* 1.1 speaks of Jesus being "baptized by John that 'all righteousness might be fulfilled'" (Matt 3:15).[5] Both *Trallians* 11.1 and *Philadelphians* 3.1 refer to those who are "not the planting of the Father" and therefore should be avoided,[6] echoing Jesus's metaphor when warning against the Pharisees: "Every plant that my heavenly Father has not planted will be uprooted" (Matt 15:13). Ignatius echoes a saying of Jesus when advising Polycarp of

3. Theophoros (God-bearer) is a cognomen (nickname). We do not know Ignatius's family name.

For a more extensive discussion of Ignatius's use of GMatthew, see Foster, "Epistles of Ignatius"; for Foster's analysis of the reception of GMatthew in Ignatius's letters, see esp. 2:173–81. A briefer although somewhat technical discussion appears in Kok, "Earliest References."

4. See Ignatius of Antioch; Schoedel, *Ignatius of Antioch*.

5. Ignatius, in Schaff, *Apostolic Fathers*, 225.

6. Ignatius, in Schaff, *Apostolic Fathers*, 195, 212.

Smyrna to be "wise as a serpent, and harmless as a dove" (*Polycarp* 2.2; Matt 10:16; Gos. Thom. 39).[7] Ignatius's expression "He that is able to receive it, let him receive it" (*Smyrnaeans* 6.1) may echo Matt 19:12d,[8] but this is more tenuous.[9] While the first example is the most exact connection between Ignatius and GMatthew, the other examples reinforce the claim that Ignatius knew and used GMatthew, which suggests that GMatthew was used in Ignatius's home church of Antioch. Since there is no evidence of Ignatius's use of any of the other canonical gospels, it appears that GMatthew was the single one favored by the Antiochene community.[10]

Canonical Developments

The *Church History* by Eusebius Pamphilus (ca. 260–339 CE), bishop of Caesarea Maritima, is the earliest extant church history (not counting the canonical book of Acts). Among other details, Eusebius provides one of the earliest lists of the books included in the biblical canon. GMatthew appears first in the New Testament, which is stated to have four gospels—the same as those viewed as canonical today. Eusebius quotes Origen of Alexandria's assertion that "among the four Gospels, which are the only indisputable ones in the Church of God under heaven, I have learned by tradition that the first was written by Matthew, who was once a publican but afterwards an apostle of Jesus Christ, and it was prepared for the converts from Judaism, and published in the Hebrew language."[11] There is no manuscript evidence to support the last claim about GMatthew having been composed in Hebrew, especially since the text throughout cites the Septuagint rather than the Hebrew Bible. Translators often infer that Origen really meant "in the Hebrew idiom," that is, in language and imagery that would make sense to a Jewish audience—a claim amply supported by both the structure and internal evidence of GMatthew itself.

7. Ignatius, in Schaff, *Apostolic Fathers*, 242.

8. Ignatius, in Schaff, *Apostolic Fathers*, 230.

9. Christine Trevett identifies thirty-six possible Ignatian cases of use of GMatthew, although only half of these have been viewed as deserving serious attention ("Approaching Matthew"). In the interests of brevity, I have kept to the handful of Ignatian texts that seem to have the most direct connections to GMatthew.

10. Concerning Ignatius's apparent ignorance of the other three canonical gospels, see Foster, "Epistles of Ignatius," 2:181–84.

11. Eusebius, *Church History* 3.11.25.4.

The canonical placement of GMatthew allows—in fact encourages—later readers to view the other gospels in relation to it. For example, Eusebius spends considerable energy in his history discussing GMatthew in comparison to the other gospels. He devotes a chapter to building on the elements of the Matthean infancy narrative that speak about Herod the Great (*Church History* 3.6.8), which provides some valuable context for reading the gospel (although contemporary readers must compensate for his naïve acceptance of the infancy narrative as entirely historical). Eusebius also provides an inventive but convoluted and so ultimately unpersuasive argument that the two genealogies in GMatthew and GLuke do not actually contradict each other, even though (among other discrepancies) they provide two different names for Jesus's paternal grandfather (3.6.7).

Because it comes first in the New Testament, contemporary readers typically elide the evidence of the other gospels to fit GMatthew. For example, we think of the Sermon on the Mount as central to "the gospel," not just GMatthew, and we add "three kings" to the Christmas crèche illustrating the nativity story in GLuke. We remember Pilate "washing his hands" of responsibility for Jesus's death and the Jerusalem mob affirming, "His blood be upon us and upon our children" (Matt 27:24–25). We remember Joseph of Arimathea burying Jesus (27:57–60) and the faithful women seeing Jesus while on the way to deliver the message of the resurrection (28:8–10). But, because GMatthew subsumes "the disciples" into "the Twelve," we do not remember that the women who followed Jesus and who carried the good news of the resurrection were "real" disciples. The bias of GMatthew even shapes our reading of the other three gospels, especially GMark, so that, for example, we subconsciously substitute "the Twelve" whenever we read the word "disciples," even though GMark clearly differentiates the two groups and includes women among Jesus's disciples. The Matthean scribes would no doubt be pleased at how successful were their efforts to replace GMark with their "new and improved" gospel, overshadowing the gospel that ended in embarrassing failure with this story they loved to tell.

Conclusions

The influence of GMatthew continues to have repercussions in the early churches beyond the one that produced this gospel. As we see in the Didache, the Matthean version of the Lord's Prayer rapidly surpassed the earlier Q version (preserved in GLuke) in the liturgical tradition. Other elements of the Sermon on the Mount become centerpieces of Christian ethics, as does the understanding of the Jesus tradition in terms of new commandments. The incorporation of this understanding of discipleship in the Great Commission scene made this kind of catechesis central to the early church, and the commission's inclusion of "all nations" justified evangelistic outreach well beyond the house of Israel to all the gentile nations known to the Greco-Roman world and eventually beyond.

In addition, the Matthean centralization of discipleship in the Twelve and the vignette about the "keys to the *basileia*" influence later church orders, which give precedence to male church leaders and provide the foundation for permanent, residential ecclesiastical leaders with the titles of bishop and deacon. The Didache recognizes itinerant prophets and teachers as having continuing importance, but their roles are restricted while the congregation is directed to provide substantial material support (essentially, tithes) to their residential leaders. This trend is continued in the letters of Ignatius of Antioch, which focus on the centrality of the community's sole bishop (the monoepiscopacy) and exhort the church members to ensure that deacons and other leaders work in harmony with the bishop's aims. The kind of authority Ignatius assigns to the bishop later develops into the monarchial episcopate, which survives to this day in churches with an episcopal polity. Such developments might have taken place without the traditions in GMatthew, but the Matthean scribes' shaping of the Jesus tradition and inclusion of special material relating to the Twelve provided ample resources for those who wanted to develop ecclesiastical structures that fit the sociopolitical expectations of the wider Greco-Roman world.

Review and Discussion Questions

A. Review Questions

1. What are some of the ways in which GMatthew influenced the early Christian communities?
2. How did GMatthew make a mark on early Christian liturgy? What is an example that we still see today?
3. What are a few of the connections between GMatthew and the views of Ignatius of Antioch?

B. Discussion Questions

1. What do you think about GMatthew's focus on the "Twelve" and its later development into the monoepiscopacy and theological claims like "apostolic succession"? Was the eventual exclusion of women from the episcopal role a logical and/or necessary outcome from GMatthew's presentation of the Twelve? How so or how not?
2. Did the Christian community lose something important when residential church leaders (bishops, presbyters, deacons) replaced itinerant preachers and prophets? How so or how not? Are there other ways in which the function of the itinerant preachers and prophets have been drawn back into the organized churches?
3. What is lost and what is gained by viewing GMatthew within the context of emerging Christian discourse? Does this approach prompt you to view GMatthew differently? How so? What do you think of that difference?

CONCLUSION

The Story We Love to Tell

THE GOSPEL ACCORDING TO Matthew conveys a story of Jesus that Christians for centuries have loved to tell. Perhaps the most frequently quoted of the canonical gospels in the first few Christian centuries, the portrayal of Jesus in GMatthew and the Matthean scribes' interpretation of Jesus's significance has had a lasting impact on Christian theology. While not the earliest of the canonical gospels, GMatthew was placed first in the New Testament canon because of this positive reception history and also because of the explicit connections GMatthew makes with "the Law and the Prophets" of the Jewish Bible.

Correcting the previous gospel in GMark, the Matthean scribes add key features to their gospel to place Jesus solidly within the history of Israel and also on the wider world stage. The infancy narrative prologue to GMatthew shows the importance of the birth of the Messiah for the Jewish people living under foreign domination, while the scene with the magi illustrates the international appeal that this Jewish Messiah will have, thus fulfilling the prophecy of Isaiah (among others) about the salvation of the entire gentile world through God's blessing to the chosen people.

The numerous wonderworks of Jesus confirm the divine authority of his message. The use of parables, allegories, beatitudes, and other concise oral forms make Jesus's teaching in GMatthew memorable and easily adapted to catechetical settings. The focus on the Twelve as a key group among the women and men disciples both reinforces the central importance of Jesus for the people of Israel and provides a framework for developing organizational structures in the early churches.

The story in GMatthew modifies that of GMark to make Jesus more confident, especially in the scene at the cross, and more accepting of the possibility that one might be a true disciple while being "poor in spirit"—that is, devoting one's funds to the use of the community—without entirely relinquishing control of those resources. Nevertheless, the Matthean Jesus is not laissez-faire about wealth: eternal punishment is promised for those who hoard their wealth, refusing to use their resources to feed the hungry, give drink to the thirsty, clothe the naked, and support the destitute in other ways.

The empty-tomb scene and post-resurrection appearances in GMatthew seem designed to build the community's confidence in the authenticity of the gospel concerning Jesus's resurrection and the divinely authorized mission of the women and men disciples of Jesus to share this astounding message, both among the people of Israel and with the wider gentile world. The success of that evangelistic mission is self-evident; within decades of the publication of this gospel, Christianity had spread throughout the Greco-Roman world, from Jerusalem to Rome and beyond. The Matthean scribes created a story people truly loved to hear and tell. Jesus's disciples continue to live and tell that story even today.

SELECT BIBLIOGRAPHY

Ahearn-Kroll, Patricia D. "Joseph and Asenath." The Torah, 2021. https://www.thetorah.com/article/joseph-and-asenath.

Augustine. "Sermon 23 on the New Testament." New Advent, 1888. Translated by R. G. MacMullen. From *NPNF*[1], edited by Philip Schaff, vol. 6 (Buffalo, NY: Christian Literature). Edited for New Advent by Kevin Knight. http://www.newadvent.org/fathers/160323.htm.

———. "Sermon 47: On the Sheep." In *Sermons 20–50*, translated by Edmund Hill, edited by John E. Rotelle, 298–326. Vol. 3.2 of *The Works of Saint Augustine: A Translation for the 21st Century*. Hyde Park, NY: New City, 1991.

———. "Sermon 73A: On the Man Who Sowed Good Seed in His Field, in the Gospel According to Matthew 13." In *Sermons 51–94*, translated by Edmund Hill, edited by John E. Rotelle, 295–98. Vol. 3.3 of *The Works of Saint Augustine: A Translation for the 21st Century*. Hyde Park, NY: New City, 1991.

Bonhoeffer, Dietrich. *The Cost of Discipleship*. Rev. ed. New York: Macmillan, 1963.

Boxall, Ian. "Matthew." In *The Jerome Biblical Commentary for the Twenty-First Century*, edited by John J. Collins et al., 1168–237. 3rd ed. London: T&T Clark, 2022.

Brooks, E. W., trans. *Joseph and Asenath: The Confession and Prayer of Asenath, Daughter of Pentephres the Priest*. London: Society for Promoting Christian Knowledge, 1918. https://archive.org/details/josephasenathconoobroo/mode/2up.

Brown, Raymond. *The Birth of the Messiah: A Commentary on the Infancy Narratives in the Gospels of Matthew and Luke*. 2 vols. AYBRL. New Haven: Yale University Press, 1999.

Buckley, Jorunn Jacobsen. *The Mandaeans: Ancient Texts and Modern People*. American Academy of Religion. Oxford: Oxford University Press, 2002.

Charlesworth, James H., and Loren T. Stuckenbruck. "Rule of the Congregation (*1Qsa*)." In *Rule of the Community and Related Documents*, edited by James H. Charlesworth et al., 108–18. Vol. 1 of *The Dead Sea Scrolls: Hebrew, Aramaic, and Greek Texts with English Translations*. Tübingen: Mohr Siebeck, 1994.

Crossan, John Dominic. "From Moses to Jesus: Parallel Themes." *BRev* 2 (1986) 18–27.

———. *Jesus: A Revolutionary Biography*. San Francisco: HarperSanFrancisco, 1994.

Culpepper, R. Alan. "Matthew and John: Reflections of Early Christianity in Relation to Judaism." In *John and Judaism: A Contested Relationship in Context*, edited by R. Alan Culpepper and Paul N. Anderson, 189–220. RBS 87. Atlanta: SBL Press, 2017.

Culpepper, R. Alan, and Paul N. Anderson, eds. *John and Judaism: A Contested Relationship in Context*. RBS 87. Atlanta: SBL Press, 2017.

Dylan, Bob. "Gotta Serve Somebody." Side 1, track 1, on *Slow Train Coming*, Columbia Records, 1979. https://www.bobdylan.com/songs/gotta-serve-somebody/.

Eusebius Pamphilus. *Church History*. Christian Classics Ethereal Library, n.d. From *NPNF*[2], edited by Philip Schaff and Henry Wace, vol. 1 (Edinburgh: T&T Clark, n.d.). https://ccel.org/ccel/schaff/npnf201/npnf201.i.html.

Foster, Paul. "The Epistles of Ignatius of Antioch and the Writings That Later Formed the New Testament." In *The Reception of the New Testament in the Apostolic Fathers*, edited by Andrew F. Gregory and Christopher M. Tuckett, 2:159–86. Oxford: Oxford University Press, 2005.

Gale, Aaron M. "God, Galilee, and the Gospels Revisited: Was Matthew Written from Bethsaida?" *Proceedings EGLBS & MWSBL* 28 (2008) 15–24.

———. "The Gospel According to Matthew: Introduction and Annotations." In *The Jewish Annotated New Testament*, edited by Amy-Jill Levine and Marc Zvi Brettler, 9–66. Oxford: Oxford University Press, 2017.

———. *Redefining Ancient Borders: The Jewish Scribal Framework of Matthew's Gospel*. Edinburgh: T&T Clark, 2005.

Garrow, Alan. *The Gospel of Matthew's Dependence on the Didache*. JSNTSup 254. Edinburgh: T&T Clark, 2004.

Glatzer, Nahum M., ed. *The Judaic Tradition*. Boston: Beacon, 1969.

Horace [Quintus Horatius Flaccus]. "Q. Horati Flacci *Carminum liber tertius*." Latin Library, n.d. https://www.thelatinlibrary.com/horace/carm3.shtml.

Hughes, Frank W. *A Guide to Mark*. Eugene, OR: Cascade, 2025.

Ignatius of Antioch. https://www.earlychristianwritings.com/ignatius.html.

Josephus [Flavius Josephus, a.k.a. Yosef ben Matityahu]. *Antiquities of the Jews*. University of Chicago, 1737. From *The Genuine Works of Flavius Josephus, the Jewish Historian*, translated by William Whiston (London: N.p.). https://penelope.uchicago.edu/josephus/.

Keddie, Tony. "Render unto Caesar." Bible Odyssey, n.d. https://www.bibleodyssey.org/articles/render-unto-caesar/.

Kloppenborg, John S. *Q, the Earliest Gospel: An Introduction to the Original Stories and Sayings of Jesus*. Louisville: Westminster John Knox, 2008.

Kok, Michael J. "The Earliest References to Matthew's Gospel: Ignatius of Antioch?" Jesus Memoirs, Jan. 18, 2023. https://jesusmemoirs.wordpress.com/2023/01/18/the-earliest-references-to-matthews-gospel-ignatius-of-antioch/.

Lake, Kirsopp, trans. "Didache: The Teaching of the Twelve Apostles." Early Christian Writings, 1912. From *The Apostolic Fathers*, LCL 24. https://www.earlychristianwritings.com/text/didache-lake.html.

Loader, William R. G. "Tensions in Matthean and Johannine Soteriology Viewed in Their Jewish Context." In *John and Judaism: A Contested Relationship in Context*, edited by R. Alan Culpepper and Paul N. Anderson, 175–880. RBS 87. Atlanta: SBL Press, 2017.

Macwilliam, Stuart. "Marriage Metaphors in the Prophets." Bible Odyssey, n.d. https://www.bibleodyssey.org/articles/marriage-metaphors-in-the-prophets/.

Maloney, Francis J. *The Shape of Matthew's Story*. Biblical Studies from the Catholic Biblical Association 12. Mahwah, NJ: Paulist, 2023.

McGinn, Sheila E. *The Jesus Movement and the World of the Early Church*. Winona, MN: Anselm Academic, 2014.

———. "Matthew's Gospel." In *Study Bible for Women: The New Testament*, edited by Catherine Clark Kroeger et al., 15–72. Grand Rapids: Baker, 1996.

———. "'Not Counting [the] Women': A Feminist Reading of Matthew 26–28." In *SBL 1995 Seminar Papers*, edited by Gene H. Lovering, 168–76. Atlanta: Scholars Press, 1995.

———. "Why Now the Women? Social-Historical Insights on Gender Roles in Matthew 26–28." *Proceedings EGLBS & MWSBL* 17 (1997) 108–35.

Naselli, Andy. "The Structural Difference Between Matthew and Mark." Andy Naselli, Dec. 30, 2010. https://andynaselli.com/matthew-and-mark.

Quintilian [Marcus Fabius Quintilianus]. *The Lesser Declamations*. Edited and translated by D. R. Shackleton Bailey. Vol. 1. LCL 500. Cambridge: Harvard University Press, 2006.

Reardon, B. P., ed. *Collected Ancient Greek Novels*. Berkeley: University of California Press, 2008.

Riddle, M. B., trans. *The Didache*. New Advent, 1886. From *ANF*, edited by Alexander Roberts et al., vol. 7 (Buffalo, NY: Christian Literature). Edited for New Advent by Kevin Knight. http://www.newadvent.org/fathers/0714.htm.

Schaff, Philip, ed. *The Apostolic Fathers with Justin Martyr and Irenaeus*. Christian Classics Ethereal Library, 1885. From *ANF*, vol. 1. https://www.ccel.org/ccel/s/schaff/anf01/cache/anf01.pdf.

Schoedel, William R. *Ignatius of Antioch: A Commentary on the Letters of Ignatius of Antioch*. Edited by Helmut Koester. Hermeneia. Minneapolis: Fortress, 1985.

Streeter, Burnett H. *The Four Gospels: A Study of Origins Treating the Manuscript Tradition, Sources, Authorship, & Dates*. London: Macmillan, 1924.

Suetonius [Gaius Suetonius Tranquillus]. *Julius. Augustus. Tiberius. Gaius Caligula*. Translated by J. C. Rolfe. Vol. 1 of *Lives of the Caesars*. LCL 31. Cambridge: Harvard University Press, 1914.

Trevett, Christine. "Approaching Matthew from the Second Century: The Under-Used Ignatian Correspondence." *JSNT* 6 (1984) 59–67. http:/doi.org/10.1177/0142064X8400602003.

USCCB. "The Corporal Works of Mercy." USCCB, n.d. https://www.usccb.org/beliefs-and-teachings/how-we-teach/new-evangelization/jubilee-of-mercy/the-corporal-works-of-mercy.

Virgil [Publius Vergilius Maro]. "Eclogue 4." The Internet Classics Archive. https://classics.mit.edu/Virgil/eclogue.4.iv.html.

Weiss, Johannes. *Jesus' Proclamation of the Kingdom of God*. Edited by Richard H. Hiers and D. Larrimore Holland. Lives of Jesus. Minneapolis: Fortress, 1971.

———. *Die Predigt Jesu vom Reiche Gottes*. Göttingen: Vandenhoeck & Ruprecht, 1892. https://archive.org/details/gtu_32400005730878.

www.ingramcontent.com/pod-product-compliance
Lightning Source LLC
LaVergne TN
LVHW090517110826
845146LV00003B/884

* 9 7 9 8 3 8 5 2 6 7 4 2 2 *